JULY 1991, NORTH ATLANTIC, SOME 300 NAUTICAL MILES WEST OF THE AZORES ARCHIPELAGO, THE USS "THEODORE ROOSEVELT" IS WRAPPING UP THE LONG SERIES OF EXERCISES THAT PRECEDE ANY OPERATIONAL DEPLOYMENT...

ALL MANNER OF MANOEUVRES FOLLOW EACH OTHER AT BREAKNECK PACE, 24 HOURS A DAY... SIMULATED ATTACKS ON LAJES AIRFIELD...

AND 150 MILES AWAY FROM THE CARRIER, CHARGING TOWARDS IT JUST ABOVE THE WAVES, THREE US AIR FORCE B-52S... EACH CARRIES A DOZEN OF THE FORMIDABLE "HARPOON" ANTI-SHIP MISSILES...

LEADER HERE, BE READY! MISSILES LAUNCH IN 12 MINUTES!

AT 27,000 FEET, THE EYE OF THE FLEET IS KEEPING WATCH: AN E-2C "HAWKEYE"...

NINE MINUTES...

AXEMAN, LOOKOUT: BANDITS BEARING ONE-FOUR-SEVEN... ALTITUDE ONE-FIVE-ZERO!

AXEMAN HERE! ROGER. GIVE ME A VECTOR FOR INTERCEPT!

HEAD ON TWO-FOUR-FIVE... DISTANCE: ZERO-EIGHT-FIVE NAUTICAL MILES...

MAJ J TUMBLER

SEVEN AND A HALF MINUTES...

THE TWO "TOMCATS" HAVE ALREADY STARTED TURNING...

... AND ENGAGE THEIR AFTERBURNERS TO GET INTO FIRING POSITION AS FAST AS POSSIBLE...

FIVE MINUTES...

AXEMAN HERE! TARGET IS CLOSE... DISTANCE: ONE-FIVE-ZERO. FIRING MY "PHOENIX"... MARK! MARK! MARK! TARGET WILL BE CONSIDERED DESTROYED IN 40 SECONDS!

FOUR MINUTES...

SUDDENLY... **HELL!** AXEMAN, LOOKOUT: I HAVE A NEW RETURN BEARING ZERO-ZERO-SIX!

AND SOON AFTER...

LOOKOUT, AXEMAN AND EVERYONE ELSE! THIS IS JOKER! IT'S THE AIR FORCE CALLING! YOU NO LONGER HAVE A CARRIER... I JUST FIRED MY 12 "HARPOONS" AT IT!

THEY'LL IMPACT IN SIX SECONDS! AND DON'T YOU COME WHINING ABOUT HOW BANDIT 14 WAS LIMITED TO THREE B-52S!

DO YOU THINK THAT THE DAY IVAN DECIDES TO COME AFTER YOUR FLOATING WINNEBAGOS...

... THEY'LL GIVE YOU THE NUMBER OF BIRDS AND THE ATTACK VECTOR?! *YEEHAH!*

A Buck Danny ADVENTURE

Drawing: FRANCIS BERGÈSE   Script: JACQUES DE DOUHET
Colour Work: FRÉDÉRIC BERGÈSE

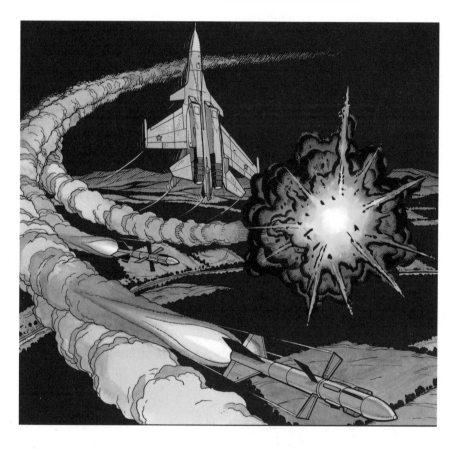

THE SECRETS
OF THE BLACK SEA

The adventures of "Buck Danny" were created by Georges Troisfontaines,
Victor Hubinon and Jean-Michel Charlier.

9th CINEBOOK
The 9th Art Publisher

Original title: Buck Danny 45 – Les secrets de la mer Noire
Original edition: © Dupuis, 1994 by Bergèse & de Douhet
www.dupuis.com

English translation: © 2009 Cinebook Ltd

Translator: Jerome Saincantin
Lettering and text layout: Imadjinn sarl
Printed in Spain by Just Colour Graphic

This edition first published in Great Britain in 2010 by
Cinebook Ltd
56 Beech Avenue
Canterbury, Kent
CT4 7TA
www.cinebook.com

A CIP catalogue record for this book
is available from the British Library

ISBN 978-1-84918-018-4

AT THAT MOMENT, ONBOARD THE VIRTUALLY SUNK "ROOSEVELT"...

CAPTAIN TUCKSON TO REPORT TO THE ADMIRAL IMMEDIATELY...

WHAT DOES HE WANT WITH ME THIS TIME?!

ANYTIME THERE'S A PROBLEM OR A CHORE, THEY CALL TUCKSON!

TUCKSON! I... ERM... HAVE THE IMMENSE PLEASURE TO ANNOUNCE THAT YOU HAVE BEEN CHOSEN AS THE MOST COMPETENT AND LIKABLE PILOT ON BOARD!

?!

GRRRR...

ER... TO BE HONEST, SIR, I'M NOT SUR-PRISED!

I AM! IT'S LIKE THEY ALL SUDDENLY BECAME INSANE... OR...

... ERM! THEY SENSED A CHORE COMING LIKE ONLY THE NAVY CAN WHIP THEM UP... ERM!... AND, ER... ANYWAY, THEY'VE MADE SURE THAT YOU'D BE THE ONE STUCK WITH IT!

?!

3A

THIS IS ABOUT A NEW PROGRAM THE ADMIRALTY WANTS TO IMPLEMENT IN ORDER TO HAVE MORE MULTI-SKILLED PILOTS, FAMILIARISED WITH THE ENTIRE GAMUT OF OUR OPERATIONS...

... FROM AIR SUPERIORITY TO ANTI-SUBMARINE WARFARE AND SEA RESCUE. THEREFORE, FOR THE NEXT 10 DAYS, YOU'LL KEEP YOUR "HORNET" PARKED AND FLY A "SEA KING," BEGINNING IMMEDIATELY! A CREW IS WAITING FOR YOU AT SQUADRON HS-9.

DISMISSED! AND WATCH IT WITH THE DOOR! FOR ONCE, SPARE ME YOUR CLOWNESQUE EXITS!

YESSIR!

GRROARF!

ME! FLY AN SH-3! THE MANIAC! AND I COULD SWEAR I SAW HIS MUG SMIRK!

... MAKES YOU WONDER WHO'S IN CHARGE, THE DOG OR THE ADMIRAL!

3B

WHAT A DISGRACE, FLYING THIS CRATE! AND TO BE TRACKING THE LAST MORON OF A SOVIET SUB SKIPPER WHO HASN'T BEEN TOLD THAT THE COLD WAR IS OVER!

THAT MORON, SIR, MUST BE DRIVING AN "AKULA"... A PARTICULARLY QUIET CLASS! NEW HEADING NOW: TWO-SIX-ZERO!

ROGER! NINETEENTH COURSE CHANGE. I KEPT COUNT!

AND HOW MUCH MORE OF THIS?...

WE'RE TO BE RELIEVED IN TWO HOURS, SIR!

TWO HOURS?! WHAT A CURSE!

GET READY, SIR...

PREPARE TO LOWER SONAR IN 10 SECONDS...

YEAH! TWENTY-FOURTH TIME!

SONAR LOWERED, SIR!

YEAH!

NOISE... NO SIGNATURE... READY, SIR... NEW HEADING!

ZERO-EIGHT-ZERO.

TWENTIETH TIME... OKAY!

SIR! THAT MORON OF YOURS IS PRETTY GOOD. AS SOON AS HE DETECTED OUR APPROACH, HE DIVED, SLOWED DOWN AND HID UNDER A POD OF SPERM WHALES THAT ARE MAKING QUITE A RACKET, WHICH IS KEEPING HIM COMPLETELY HIDDEN FROM OUR SONAR!

AH! THE WHALES ARE ON THEIR SIDE NOW! WELL, THAT'S JUST PEACHY!

THE NEXT MORNING...

A PITY YOU'RE LEAVING US IN THE MIDDLE OF THE EXERCISE, BUCK!

IT IS, ADMIRAL... ESPECIALLY FOR SOME MEET-AND-GREET IN WASHINGTON!

RATHER STRANGE, THIS DIRECT SUMMONS FROM THE CNO(*)... ESPECIALLY TWO WEEKS BEFORE OUR DEPARTURE FOR THE MEDITERRANEAN...

(*)Chief of Naval Operations

AFTER A QUIET FLIGHT, THE "HORNET" LANDS AT LANGLEY AIR FORCE BASE...

COLONEL DANNY? GOOD MORNING, SIR! I'M TO TAKE YOU TO ADMIRAL FARRELL IMMEDIATELY.

TO THE CNO, AND STEP ON IT!

THAT'S HOW HE IS! SINCE HE WAS NAMED TO THE POST, HEADQUARTERS IS LIKE AN ERUPTING VOLCANO! PEOPLE CALL HIM "PINATUBO"(*)!

(*)Volcano located in the Philippines that destroyed Clark AFB in 1991

LATER, AT THE PENTAGON...

SIT DOWN, DANNY... SORRY TO RUSH YOU! SAY... NOT A VERY GOOD DAY FOR THE "TEDDY,"(*) YESTERDAY! LET'S RECOUNT YOUR BOYS' EXPLOITS...

(*)Nickname for the USS "Theodore Roosevelt"

THE AIR FORCE IS CLAIMING THAT IT SANK THE "TEDDY," A SOVIET SUBMARINE GAVE US THE SLIP, THE PASSENGERS OF A SWISS CHARTER PLANE WERE TERRORIZED IN THE AZORES!...

HERE'S THE CONSUL'S PROTEST! AND FINALLY, AFTER YOU LEFT THIS MORNING, AN F-18 CRASHED AT SEA!

ADM. JAMES A. FARRELL

DON'T WORRY. JAMESON, THE PILOT, IS UNHARMED.

ALL THIS WOULDN'T BE THAT IMPORTANT IF THE PRESS HADN'T SUNK ITS TEETH INTO IT... I CAN ALREADY SEE TOMORROW'S HEADLINES!

The Navy in the hot seat

DISORDER IN THE NAVY

Japan Ho

Herald INTERNATIONAL Tribune

Is Our Navy Obsolete?

IN THREE WEEKS I WILL BE APPEARING BEFORE THE SENATE TO DEFEND OUR CARRIER BUDGET... CONGRESS, THE PRESS, PUBLIC OPINION ARE AGAINST US. ONLY THE PRESIDENT BACKS US UP. AND AFTER A DAY LIKE TODAY, WHAT ARGUMENTS DO I HAVE LEFT? FORTUNATELY, THERE ARE STILL...

... THE SOVIETS!

???... THE... THE SOVIETS!?

THEY'VE LAUNCHED A MASSIVE CARRIER PROGRAM... LIKE WE HAVEN'T SEEN SINCE THE JAPANESE!

THE FIRST ONE, THE "KUZNETSOV," IS UNDERGOING TRIALS AT SEA. TWO MORE ARE UNDER CONSTRUCTION, AND THEY'VE ISSUED A PRELIMINARY ORDER FOR A FOURTH!

ACCORDING TO ONI(*), FOUR MORE COULD BE IN THE PLANS! NICE SHIPS, BUCK! ONE THOUSAND FEET LONG, 65,000 TONNES, A MATCH FOR THE "FORRESTAL" CLASS. TAKE A LOOK!

BZZZZZZ

(*)Office of Naval Intelligence

THEY CAN CARRY 60 AIRCRAFT, ALL OF MORE RECENT DESIGN THAN OUR "TOMCATS" AND "INTRUDERS"!

THEIR AIR GROUPS WOULD COME CLOSE TO THE LEVEL OF OURS. IN SHORT, THEIR GOAL IS CLEAR: TO ACQUIRE A NAVAL AIR FORCE AT LEAST THE EQUAL OF OURS IN THE NEAR FUTURE! CAN YOU GRASP THE POLITICAL AND MILITARY CONSEQUENCES?!

6A

WE MUST AWAKEN PUBLIC OPINION! OBTAIN EVERY POSSIBLE BIT OF INFORMATION, TURN CONGRESS AROUND, AND, WITH PRESSURE FROM A WORRIED PUBLIC, OBTAIN OUR BUDGET FUNDING!

MiG-29 Fulcrum

Su-27 Flanker

371

DAMN IVAN! I'LL NEVER UNDERSTAND THEM... THEY CAN'T STOP HARPING ABOUT PEACE AND DISARMAMENT, AND AT THE SAME TIME THEY THROW DOWN THIS ENORMOUS GAUNTLET!

I'M CONVINCED THEY'RE CHEATING! THEY'RE TRYING TO LURE US TO SLEEP, ALL THE WHILE WORKING ON THE MOST DEVIOUS SCHEMES! THEY'VE NEVER BUILT AS MANY SHIPS AS THIS YEAR! WE'RE COUNTING ON YOU TO DISCOVER MORE ABOUT ALL THIS, SINCE THEY'RE INVITING YOU ABOARD THE "KUZNETSOV"!...

?! ME?...

YOU'RE WELL KNOWN, BUCK! MORE THAN YOU THINK! SO, AS PART OF "GLASNOST" AND THE NEW SPIRIT OF TRUST THEY'RE TRYING TO ESTABLISH WITH US, THEY'VE INVITED A DELEGATION FROM CONGRESS TO VISIT THEIR MAIN MILITARY INSTALLATIONS, INCLUDING SEBASTOPOL AND THE BLACK SEA FLEET. UNOFFICIALLY, THEIR NAVAL ATTACHÉ HAS LET ME KNOW THAT HE WOULD LIKE YOU TO BE PRESENT AMONG THE DELEGATION!

WHY? NO IDEA! BUT IF YOU ACCEPT, HE PROMISED HE'D GET YOU ONBOARD THE "KUZNETSOV" FOR A WEEK...

6B

WHAT A FABULOUS OPPORTUNITY! THE PRESIDENT IS MOST INTERESTED, AND CONSIDERS IT OF THE UTMOST IMPORTANCE: OUR BEST SPECIALIST ONBOARD THEIR MOST MODERN SHIP!

WE HAVE DEFINED THE THREE LAYERS OF SECURITY YOU'LL HAVE AT YOUR DISPOSAL... FIRST: WE HAVE SOME EXCELLENT AGENTS ON STATION; A NETWORK OF UKRAINIAN NATIONALISTS.

GOD ONLY KNOWS HOW THEY INFILTRATED THE COMMAND STRUCTURE OF THAT FLEET! IN CASE OF TROUBLE, THEY'LL CONTACT YOU UNDER THE CODENAME "NIKOLAYEV 17."

SECOND: WE'LL HAVE A DESTROYER IN THE BLACK SEA... YOUR WINGMEN TUMBLER AND TUCKSON WILL BE ABOARD WITH TWO "BLACKHAWK" HELICOPTERS IN SPECIAL OPS CONFIGURATION, READY TO EXTRACT YOU AT ANY TIME.

AND FINALLY, THIRD: THIS MINIATURE EMITTER LINKED TO THE FLEETSATCOM(*) NETWORK. TO WARN US IN CASE OF TROUBLE, PRESS THE BUTTON!

(*)Fleet Satellite Communications: US Navy satellite network

IT'S WATERPROOF AND IT FLOATS. THE SIGNAL IT EMITS LASTS FOR THREE MINUTES AND INDICATES POSITION WITHIN A 50-FOOT RADIUS. KEEP IT WITH YOU AT ALL TIMES!

WHAT IF THE RUSSIANS SEARCH ME?

OUT OF THE QUESTION! THE DIPLOMATIC STATUS THEY'VE ACCORDED YOU FORBIDS IT. HOWEVER, SINCE THEIR BRASS SEEM SOMEWHAT DIVIDED ON THIS, YOU'LL TRAVEL AS A CIVILIAN...

... UNDER A FALSE IDENTITY. YOU'LL BE FLETCHER EVANS, ASSISTANT TO SENATOR SMIGHT AND ENGINEER FOR GRUMMAN.

BUT, ADMIRAL, I'M NOT A SPY!

WHO SAID ANYTHING ABOUT SPYING?! YOU'LL BE A COMPLETELY OFFICIAL GUEST OF THE SOVIET GOVERNMENT!

HMMM...! AND WHAT IF THEY WANTED THEIR REVENGE FOR THE UCHINSKI BUSINESS(*)?

(*)See The Aggressors.

IMPOSSIBLE! WE KNOW THEY'RE STILL LOOKING! THE SECRET OF HIS DISAPPEARANCE WAS WELL KEPT!

WHY ME? I'M STILL CONVINCED THIS INVITATION IS A TRAP!

MAYBE... IF YOU'RE WORRIED, YOU CAN STILL SAY NO!

ADMIRAL, YOU'RE CHEATING!

SO YOU AGREE! I KNEW IT! WELL DONE! THE DELEGATION LEAVES IN SIX WEEKS. BY THEN, ALL OUR PREPARATIONS WILL BE MADE.

TWO WEEKS LATER, IN THE BLACK SEA...

I DON'T LIKE THIS MISSION, TUMB!

ME, NEITHER... I'M WORRIED ABOUT BUCK!

MEANWHILE, ON THE WESTERN EDGE OF SOVIET AIRSPACE...

MR EVANS... MY ESTEEMED ASSISTANT... IN MY ROLE AS "COVER" FOR YOUR ENDEAVOURS, I SALUTE IN YOU ANOTHER VICTIM OF ADMIRAL FARRELL! BETWEEN OURSELVES, WE CALL HIM FAREWELL!

UNITED STATES OF AMERICA

WHAT DO YOU MEAN, SENATOR?

FAREWELL, YOU SEE, IS A MAN FROM ANOTHER ERA: THAT OF THE COLD WAR, WHICH DOMINATED HIS ENTIRE CAREER... FORTUNATELY, A BYGONE ERA! HE UNDERSTANDS NOTHING ABOUT THE TIMES AHEAD OF US!

HE GRASPS NEITHER THE EXHAUSTION NOR THE LOW SPIRITS OF THE RUSSIANS... AND EVEN LESS THEIR SINCERITY!

YET THEY STILL BUILD TWICE AS MANY PLANES AS WE DO! AND THEN, WHY THOSE CARRIERS, DO YOU THINK?

AUTOMATIC REFLEX... PURE INERTIA! BUT I'M AFRAID YOUR MISSION MIGHT BRING ABOUT COMPLICATIONS THAT COULD CONTRIBUTE TO THE RENEWAL OF SUCH PRODUCTION!...

DO EXPLAIN!

I WILL GIVE YOU TWO ESSENTIAL PIECES OF INFORMATION. DO WITH THEM AS YOU SEE FIT...

I KNOW FROM A TRUSTED SOURCE THAT FARRELL'S RUSSIAN COUNTERPARTS INTEND TO CAPTURE YOU AND REVEAL YOUR TRUE IDENTITY... THEY'LL ACCUSE GORBACHEV(*) OF COVERING, IF NOT INITIATING, AN ESPIONAGE MISSION AT THE HIGHEST LEVEL!

(*)Then President of the Soviet Union

TO BRING HIM DOWN?

PRECISELY! AND I CAN ASSURE YOU THAT NIKOLAYEV 17 NEVER EXISTED OUTSIDE FAREWELL'S IMAGINATION! YOU WERE MANIPULATED!

THEREFORE, AND I'M SORRY, IT IS NECESSARY THAT WE HAVE NO FURTHER CONTACT. LOOK! THIS IS THE TRAP INTO WHICH FAREWELL THREW YOU!

RAMSKOYE, 25 MILES FROM MOSCOW: A MASSIVE AERONAUTIC COMPLEX, A DENSE NETWORK OF HANGARS, STRIPS, TAXIWAYS... PARALLEL LINES OF MIG-29S, SUKHOI 24S AND 27S, TUPOLEV 160S, ILYUCHIN 76S... AS FAR AS THE EYE CAN SEE!

TROUBLING, ISN'T IT? ONE LAST THING: KNOW THAT I FORMALLY DISAPPROVE OF THIS MISSION AND THAT WITHOUT THE CNO'S INSISTENCE AND CLOUT, I'D NEVER HAVE PLAYED THIS ROLE!

SOME LONG MINUTES LATER, DURING THE INEVITABLE AND LONG-WINDED WELCOMING SPEECH...

... AND OVER TIME, THE RAPPROCHEMENT OF OUR TWO GREAT PEOPLES WILL USHER IN A NEW ERA OF PEACE...

... AND PROSPERITY, NOT ONLY FOR US, BUT FOR THE WHOLE WORLD...

... FOR AFRICA...

WHAT TO THINK?... I DON'T TRUST SENATOR SMIGHT ONE BIT, BUT I CAN'T RULE OUT SOME SCHEME BY THAT OLD FOX FARRELL, EITHER!

WHAT TO DO?... EVERY HOUR SPENT AWAY FROM THE "KUZNETSOV" ACCOMPLISHES NOTHING FOR MY MISSION AND INCREASES THE LIKELIHOOD OF A TRAP...

... FOR ASIA...

I MUST FIND A WAY TO GET MYSELF TRANSFERRED TO THE CARRIER AS SOON AS POSSIBLE... I WON'T BE ANY SAFER THERE, BUT AT LEAST I'LL BE DOING WHAT I'VE BEEN ORDERED TO...

... FOR SOUTH AMERICA...

WHOMM

OUR PRIORITY MUST BE TO PUT AN END TO THE ARMS RA...?!

?!

TO THE SURPRISE OF EVERYONE PRESENT, THE "RUSSIAN KNIGHTS"(*) PROCEED WITH THEIR AERIAL DEMONSTRATION, DROWNING OUT THE OFFICIAL SPEECH UNDER THE DIN OF THEIR ENGINES...

BRAOW

(*)Aerobatic patrol flying Su-27s

HURRAY! LONG LIVE ETERNAL RUSSIA! LONG LIVE THE RUSSIAN KNIGHTS! WATCH, MR AMERICAN... TO WELCOME YOU, THEY ARE SHOWING YOU OUR MOST BEAUTIFUL, OUR TRUEST! AND ALSO HOW MUCH WE CAN NO LONGER STAND OFFICIAL RHETORIC! I NEVER THOUGHT I'D SEE THIS!

ME, NEITHER!

I AM CAPTAIN IGOR ALEXENKO, NAVAL AVIATION, BLACK SEA FLEET!

FLETCHER EVANS, ASSISTANT TO SENATOR SMIGHT.

BY ALL THE DEMONS OF THE STEPPE! WHAT A COINCIDENCE! YOU'RE PRECISELY THE REASON I'M HERE!

ADMIRAL FRONDZE SENT ME TO FLY YOU TO THE "KUZNETSOV" AT THE EARLIEST. NO POINT IN STICKING AROUND FOR SS-20 MISSILES OR T-72 TANKS! AN SU-27 IS WAITING FOR US!

VERY WELL. YOU UNDERSTAND, OF COURSE, THAT I HAVE TO CONSULT WITH MY DELEGATION FIRST!

OF COURSE! AFTERWARDS, HAVE SOMEONE TAKE YOU TO THE NAVAL AVIATION MESS HALL. I'LL BE WAITING FOR YOU THERE...

AN HOUR LATER, AFTER HAVING CONTACTED WASHINGTON AND RECEIVED THE GREEN LIGHT BY A SECURE RADIO LINK FROM THE BOEING 707, BUCK HAS JOINED IGOR ALEXENKO...

WHAT A PLEASURE TO BE ABLE TO SKIP THE RECEPTION AT THE EMBASSY!

NO KIDDING!

HEADING 190...WE WILL FLY OVER OREL, POLTAVA AND KHERSON.

HALFWAY THROUGH THE FLIGHT, WE WILL REFUEL FROM AN IL-76, THEN COME TO LOW ALTITUDE FOR AN EXERCISE WITH SOME MIG-29S FROM THE PVO-STRANY(*) WHO WILL ATTEMPT TO INTERCEPT US!

(*)Soviet Air Defence arm

THAT'S SOME PROGRAM, CAPTAIN! I'M REALLY GLAD TO HAVE LEFT MOSCOW!

I DON'T DOUBT IT! WOULD YOU LIKE ME TO SHOW YOU WHAT THIS PLANE CAN DO? AFTER ALL, I IMAGINE THAT'S ALSO WHY YOU CAME!?

TO BE COMPLETELY HONEST, YES, IT IS!

OK, HOLD ON!

THE SU-27 LAUNCHES INTO A VERTIGINOUS SERIES OF REVOLUTIONS. BARREL ROLLS, LOOPS, IMMELMANNS...

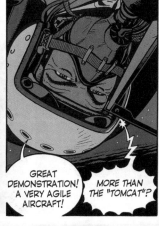

GREAT DEMONSTRATION! A VERY AGILE AIRCRAFT!

MORE THAN THE "TOMCAT"?

YOU'LL UNDERSTAND IF I DON'T ANSWER THIS QUESTION!

COMPLETELY! BUT YOU HAVEN'T SEEN ANYTHING YET!

11A

THE GRAND FINALE: PUGACHEV'S "COBRA"!

CONCEIVED BY VIKTOR PUGACHEV, TEST PILOT OF THE SU-27, AND MADE POSSIBLE BY THE EXCEPTIONAL WEIGHT/THRUST RATIO OF THE AIRCRAFT, THE "COBRA" MANOEUVRE CONSISTS OF INSTANTLY LOSING 200 TO 300 MPH BY A VIOLENT NOSE-UP, FOLLOWED BY A RECOVERY AND RE-ACCELERATION.

WHOO! YOU HAVE A HECK OF A WAY OF ANSWERING YOUR OWN QUESTIONS!

AND YOU TAKE GS PRETTY WELL, MR EVANS!

THAT INDICATES A LONG HABIT! BY THE WAY, MAY I CALL YOU FLETCHER? CALL ME IGOR!

FLETCH WILL DO EVEN BETTER!

I WAS A PILOT IN THE NAVY AND TOOK PART IN THE DEVELOPMENT OF THE F-14 AS A TEST PILOT... BUT MY FILE MUST HAVE FOUND ITS WAY INTO YOUR HANDS, MUSTN'T IT?

INDEED, B... ER... FLETCH! BUT, EXCUSE ME: I MUST CONCENTRATE ON THE REFUELLING MANOEUVRE!

11B

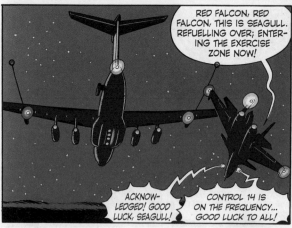

RED FALCON, RED FALCON, THIS IS SEAGULL. REFUELLING OVER; ENTERING THE EXERCISE ZONE NOW!

ACKNOWLEDGED! GOOD LUCK, SEAGULL!

CONTROL 14 IS ON THE FREQUENCY... GOOD LUCK TO ALL!

THE FOUR MIGS ARE GUIDED BY THREE GROUND RADAR STATIONS. CONTROL 14 IS KHERSON'S STATION, AND IT'S COORDINATING THE DATA.

THE AREA IS VERY HILLY; WE'LL FLY ACROSS IT DOWN IN THE VALLEYS. THEY DON'T STAND A CHANCE OF DETECTING US. MOREOVER, SINCE THIS SYSTEM FORCES THEM TO BE CHATTY, I'LL GET ON THEIR FREQUENCY!

THAT'S A BIT OUTSIDE THE RULES, IGOR!

ANY TACTIC IMPLIES EXPLOITING THE ENEMY'S WEAKNESSES! AND DON'T FORGET: I'M DEFENDING THE NAVY'S HONOUR!

THAT'S FAIR ENOUGH! ONE LAST QUESTION: THE MIG-29 IS SAID TO BE EQUIPPED WITH A "LOOK-DOWN" RADAR... WON'T THEY SEE US!?

NOT IF WE FLY LOW ENOUGH... OUR SMALL RETURN WILL BLEND IN WITH THE TERRAIN. BESIDES, AIR DEFENCE PILOTS ARE USELESS! YOU'LL SEE; IT'LL GO WITHOUT A HITCH!

AND, JUST AS IGOR PREDICTED...

RED FALCON 1 TO CONTROL 14... ARE YOU PEOPLE ASLEEP?! YOU HAVEN'T GIVEN US ANYTHING IN SIX MINUTES!

RED FALCON, THIS IS CONTROL 14. STATION 16 HAD A WEAK, SPORADIC CONTACT, BUT THEY LOST IT... GO TAKE A LOOK HEADING 216, JUST IN CASE...

THIS IS RED FALCON 3... "JUST IN CASE"?! ARE YOU KIDDING ME, CONTROL 14?!

SUDDENLY, THE SUKHOI'S RADAR DETECTOR WAILS...

EEEEEEEE

BY THE DEVIL! THEY'VE DETECTED US! I WONDER HOW THEY MANAGED IT... UNLESS...

RED FALCON, THIS IS BREJNEV 3! I HAVE YOUR SEAGULL! HERE ARE YOUR VECTORS: RED 1, HEADING 240, 300 MILES. RED 3...

FALCON 1 AND 3 HERE, THANK YOU! BUT IT'S TOO LATE. THANKS TO CONTROL 14, WE'RE TOO FAR AWAY. WE'RE HEADING BACK TO BASE!

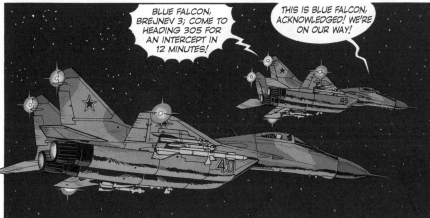

BLUE FALCON, BREJNEV 3; COME TO HEADING 305 FOR AN INTERCEPT IN 12 MINUTES!

THIS IS BLUE FALCON, ACKNOWLEDGED! WE'RE ON OUR WAY!

THEY BROUGHT IN A "COMPASS 50"—AN AWACS, AS YOU CALL THEM... THEY'VE ALSO SWITCHED FREQUENCIES, AND I CAN'T FIND THE NEW ONE!

13A

THAT'S FAIR ENOUGH TOO! THEY'RE NOT AS USELESS AS YOU THOUGHT!

STILL, IT'S STRANGE... EVERY DETAIL OF THIS EXERCISE WAS PREPARED IN ADVANCE, AND WHAT'S HAPPENING WASN'T PLANNED! IN OUR COUNTRY, THIS TYPE OF IMPROVISATION IS SOMEWHAT SURPRISING!

IT'S UNTHINKABLE WITHOUT A SERIOUS REASON AND THE PROTECTION OF A HIGHER AUTHORITY! GUIDED BY A "COMPASS," THE MIG WILL FIND US EASILY! I'LL TRY SOMETHING ELSE!

IF THE AEROFLOT FLIGHT FROM KIEV TO SEBASTOPOL IS ON TIME, WE SHOULD BE A FEW MINUTES FROM IT... I'LL GET CLOSE ENOUGH TO MERGE OUR RADAR CONTACT WITH THE AIRLINER'S. THEY WON'T DARE TAKE THIS ANY FURTHER!

WHAT ARE YOU AFRAID OF, IGOR?

I DON'T KNOW FOR SURE, BUT MY INSTINCTS ARE TELLING ME WE SHOULD BE READY FOR ANYTHING... MY COUNTRY IS GOING THROUGH A TROUBLED PERIOD, WHEN ANYTHING CAN HAPPEN. DARK FORCES ARE AT WORK. WE MUSTN'T TAKE ANY CHANCES...

13B

MEANWHILE... BLUE FALCON, BREJNEV 3; THEY'VE TURNED AND ARE CLIMBING; THIS IS YOUR NEW HEADING...

THANKS, BREJNEV, BUT NO NEED... WE'VE JUST ACQUIRED THEM ON OUR OWN RADAR!

ABOARD THE SUKHOI, THE ALARM SOUNDS A SECOND TIME...

EEEEEEEE

DAMMIT! THE MIG ON OUR 9 O'CLOCK! WE'LL NEVER HAVE TIME TO CATCH UP WITH THE AIRLINER!

ALL WE CAN DO NOW IS TRY TO SHAKE THEM... I'M COMING BACK TO A 190 HEADING AND DIVING AT FULL POWER!

BLUE FALCON, THIS IS BREJNEV 3... SEAGULL HAS JUST CHANGED HEADING AGAIN... IS ACCELERATING! HE'S GOING TO GET AWAY FROM YOU!... EXECUTE PROCEDURE K! I REPEAT...

WHAT?! SHOOT DOWN SEAGULL?! ARE YOU CRAZY?!

BLUE FALCON, BREJNEV 3. THE ORDER IS CONFIRMED AND AUTHENTICATED! EXECUTE PROCEDURE K!

14A

THEN THEY'RE THE ONES WHO'VE LOST THEIR MINDS! HAVE IT RECONFIRMED AND RE-AUTHENTICATED!

OK... BUT YOU'RE TAKING A BIG RISK!

WE'RE GAINING ON THEM... A FEW MORE MINUTES AND I THINK WE'LL BE OUT OF RANGE OF THEIR MISSILES!

YOU'RE GIVING ME THE IMPRESSION THAT THESE EXERCISES INCLUDE LIVE WEAPON FIRE! AM I RIGHT?...

BLUE FALCON 2 HERE. SEAGULL'S STILL IN MISSILE RANGE ON MY FIRE CONTROL RADAR! BUT IT MIGHT NOT BE FOR MUCH LONGER!

AFFIRMATIVE... ARM YOUR TWO R-27S!

BEEEP BEEEP BEEE BEEEP

THE MISSILES' TARGETING SYSTEMS HAVE LOCKED ONTO US! THE EXERCISE IS OVER... AT LEAST, IT'S SUPPOSED TO BE!...

BLUE FALCON, BREJNEV 3. MINISTER PUGO HAS JUST CONFIRMED PROCEDURE K! COMRADES! ON YOUR LIFE, EXECUTE!

ACKNOWLEDGED, BREJNEV 3. EXECUTING. FIRE!

14B

TEEOOEEOOEE OOEEOOEEEOOEEE

NO! THEY DARED!... THEY OPENED FIRE!

OUR AIRCRAFT IS A TRAINING VERSION. IT DOESN'T HAVE ANY DECOYS OR COUNTER-MEASURE SYSTEM... I'M GOING NAP-OF-THE-EARTH AGAIN... MAYBE WE CAN PUT SOME HILLS BETWEEN THE MISSILES AND US!

15A

NO LUCK... THE GROUND IS TOO FLAT HERE FOR US TO HAVE A HOPE OF CONFUSING THOSE DAMNED GUIDANCE SYSTEMS!

I'LL BANK LEFT... THAT WAY WE'LL HAVE A BETTER CHANCE OF SEEING THEM COME. I'M COUNTING ON YOU, FLETCH! WARN ME AS SOON AS YOU SEE THEM!

FOR THE MOMENT, I HAVE NOTHING...

THERE THEY ARE! SEVEN O'CLOCK— FOUR OF THEM!

GIVE ME A SIGNAL WHEN YOU THINK THEY'RE ONE NAUTICAL MILE FROM US. IT'S OUR LAST CHANCE!

ALMOST... NOW!

Francis Bergèse

15B

INSTANTLY, IGOR PULLS THE SUKHOI INTO ANOTHER "COBRA." WITH THEIR VELOCITY SUDDENLY MUCH TOO HIGH, THE MISSILES CANNOT CURVE THEIR TRAJECTORY SHARPLY ENOUGH TO SCORE A HIT... BUT THE PROXIMITY FUSE OF THE CLOSEST ONE TRIGGERS ITS EXPLOSION...

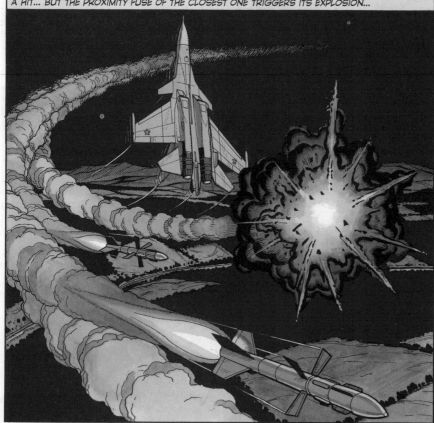

GOSH!... IGOR! ARE YOU OK?...

I'M FINE... BUT THAT WAS QUITE A JOLT! ARE WE STILL FLYING?!

I RECOVERED FROM THE BEGINNING OF A SPIN... YOU HAVE THE STICK!

BY MARX'S BEARD, THAT WAS TOO CLOSE!... SYSTEMS ARE UNDAMAGED, THE FIRE IS OUT...

YOU'RE AN ACE, IGOR! I DON'T KNOW ANY PILOT WHO COULD HAVE DONE BETTER!

I DO!... ONE OF YOUR COUNTRYMEN... AND YOU KNOW HIM: BUCK DANNY!

18

FALCON, BREJNEV 3. WHAT ARE YOU WAITING FOR?! SEAGULL IS GETTING AWAY! **PROCEDURE K! EXECUTE!**

HE MANAGED TO EVADE OUR R-27S! BUT NOW WE'RE IN R-60(*) RANGE... BLUE FALCON 1 TO BLUE 2, READY TWO R-60S FOR IMMEDIATE FIRING!

(*)Short-range missiles (maximum six miles)

TEEOOOO

HELL! HERE THEY GO AGAIN!

I DON'T THINK WE'LL MAKE IT THIS TIME!

HAVE YOU SEEN THE DAMAGE ON THE RIGHT WING? I DOUBT IT'D ALLOW US ANOTHER "COBRA"!...

YOU'RE RIGHT... WE HAVE NO CHOICE BUT TO PUNCH OUT. GET READY!

TO BE HONEST WITH YOU, I'VE BEEN PREPARING FOR THIS EVENTUALITY FOR A WHILE NOW! I'M READY!

GO!

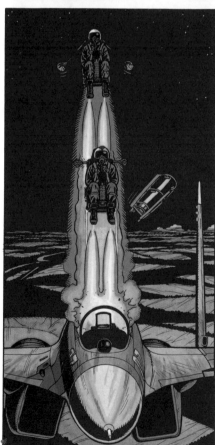

AND A FEW SECONDS LATER...

WHO ARE THEY?

OUR ENEMIES... ASSASSINS WHO'VE COME TO FINISH WHAT THE MIGS STARTED! AS FOR WHO SENT THEM, I HAVE TOO MANY HYPOTHESES... IN OTHER WORDS, NO CLEAR IDEA!

SUDDENLY...

BAOOM

!

ONE OF THE MIGS BLEW UP!

LOOK! THEY'RE RUNNING AWAY!

THIS IS ALBATROSS LEADER... I'VE LOCATED THEM!

HURRAY! THOSE ARE OUR PEOPLE! FLETCH, YOU HAVE JUST WITNESSED A HISTORICAL EVENT: THE FIRST AIR COMBAT BETWEEN SOVIET AIRCRAFT! OUR NAVY SHOT THIS FASCIST DOWN!

WRONG, IGOR! THE FIRST COMBAT WAS OURS! YOUR BUDDIES ONLY EVENED THE SCORE AT 1-1!

THAT'S TRUE! WHAT WAS I THINKING?... I SUPPOSE A PILOT WOULD RATHER FORGET HE'S BEEN SHOT DOWN!

AFTER A LONG WAIT UNDER THE PROTECTION OF THE SU-27 PATROL, THE TWO PILOTS ARE PICKED UP BY A NAVY HELICOPTER...

AS YOU KNOW, IGOR, FOR SOME TIME NOW, THE ADMIRAL HAS MADE US LISTEN SYSTEMATICALLY TO MESSAGES TRANSMITTED OVER CERTAIN SUPPOSEDLY SECRET FREQUENCIES...

... INCLUDING THAT OF THE AIR DEFENCE. HE MUST HAVE BEEN EXPECTING SOMETHING TO HAPPEN, BECAUSE HE PUT US ON ALERT AS SOON AS THE "COMPASS" TOOK OFF... AND THE ORDER TO TAKE OFF OURSELVES FOLLOWED SOON AFTER!

THE OTHERS WERE SO CHATTY THAT THE "KUZNETSOV" HAD NO TROUBLE GUIDING US TOWARDS THE MIGS THAT WERE INTERCEPTING YOU!

WHO FLEW THE SUKHOIS?

COTLENKO AND TUMBLER!

?!... TUMBLER?

SURPRISED? IT'S TRUE THAT THIS IS HARDLY A RUSSIAN-SOUNDING NAME!

HE'S A VOLGA GERMAN(*)... ONE OF THE FEW WHO MANAGED TO INTEGRATE FULLY... TO THE POINT THAT HE MADE IT INTO OUR NAVY... AN EXCEPTIONAL PILOT!

(*) In the 18th century, at the invitation of Catherine II of Russia, a colony of 27,000 Germans settled along the Volga. There was never any real integration.

LATER...

WE'RE NEAR THE COAST... NOTHING CAN HAPPEN TO US NOW, MY DEAR FLETCH!

I HOPE YOU'RE RIGHT!

ONE THING BEFORE WE LAND: ONCE ABOARD, YOU'LL DISCOVER BEHAVIOURS YOU'RE UNUSED TO ONBOARD YOUR OWN SHIPS...

AFTER TONIGHT, I DON'T SEE WHAT COULD SURPRISE ME ANYMORE!

DON'T JUDGE US ON THOSE DETAILS! OUR COUNTRY HAS BEEN IN A VERY SERIOUS CRISIS SINCE '85, WHICH HASN'T SPARED THE FLEET WE BELONG TO... NONETHELESS, THE "KUZNETSOV" IS A GOOD SHIP WITH A GOOD CREW. SHE'LL DO GREAT THINGS!

AT LAST...

GLASTOV 3, YOU HAVE LANDING CLEARANCE... WIND'S ALONG THE AXIS; SPEED IS 32 KNOTS...

WELCOME ABOARD, MR EVANS! AFTER THIS... ER... SOMEWHAT EVENTFUL NIGHT, ADMIRAL FRONDZE THOUGHT THAT A FEW HOURS OF REST WOULD DO YOU GOOD...

VERY MUCH SO, THANK YOU.

THEREFORE, HE'S POSTPONING THE PLEASURE OF MEETING YOU UNTIL DINNER. I'LL TAKE YOU TO YOUR CABIN!

COME ON, COME ON, STEP ASIDE! LET US THROUGH!

YOUR LUGGAGE WILL ARRIVE IN THE MORNING ON A HELICOPTER. IN THE MEANTIME, YOU'LL FIND EVERYTHING YOU NEED IN THE LOCKER. A MEAL WILL BE BROUGHT TO YOU. I'LL COME TO PICK YOU UP AT 18.45... GET SOME REST!

AND, AT PRECISELY 19.00 IN THE ADMIRAL'S LOUNGE...

WELCOME TO COLONEL DANNY
LONG LIVE SOVIET-AMERICAN FRIENDSHIP

COME IN, COLONEL DANNY! AND YOU, TOO, IGOR!

23

WE OWE YOU SOME APOLOGIES, COLONEL! WE'VE KNOWN YOUR REAL IDENTITY FROM THE BEGINNING... BUT THIS DECEPTION WAS NECESSARY TO ALLOW YOU TO COME!

AND AS FOR TONIGHT'S EVENTS... I'M STILL WAITING FOR AN EXPLANATION FOR THEM... I PROMISE WE WILL SPEAK OF THEM AGAIN.

PLEASE BE SEATED... AGAINST TRADITION, I PLACED YOU ON MY LEFT, BECAUSE MY RIGHT EAR ISN'T WORTH MUCH ANYMORE AND I'M TOO EAGER TO LISTEN TO YOU!

BESIDES, THAT WAY I'LL BE FREE OF THE GRUMBLING AND OBJECTIONS OF OUR POLITICAL OFFICER!... WE ALL HAVE A GREAT MANY QUESTIONS TO ASK YOU, SOME OF THEM NO DOUBT INDISCREET...

JUST SEND US PACKING IF THAT'S THE CASE! WE WON'T BE INSULTED, DON'T YOU WORRY! YOU'RE AMONG FRIENDS HERE... EXCEPT MAYBE THAT ONE... AND THEN AGAIN, MAYBE NOT!

FOR 50 YEARS, YOUR GREAT NAVY, WHICH WE ALL ENVY, HAS BEEN OPENING A PATH THAT WE SOVIET SAILORS ARE ENDEAVOURING TO FOLLOW... IT IS AN HONOUR AND A PLEASURE, COLONEL, TO WELCOME YOU ABOARD!

FIVE HOURS LATER...

WELCOME TO COLONEL DANNY
LONG LIVE SOVIET-AMERICAN FRIENDSHIP

... AT THAT MOMENT, TUMBLER, ISOLATED, HAD ONLY ONE SOLUTION LEFT TO HIM: TO THROW HIS "CORSAIR II" AGAINST THE TERRORISTS' "TOMCAT" WHILE EJECTING AT THE LAST MOMENT, WHICH HE MANAGED TO DO WITH HIS USUAL COMPOSURE(*)!

(*)See Fire from Heaven.

THANK YOU, COLONEL! YOU'VE KEPT US ALL CAPTIVATED! BUT ALLOW AN OLD RUSSIAN ADMIRAL TO REMIND YOU THAT YOU WILL HAVE A BUSY DAY TOMORROW, AND SO WILL MY YOUNG OFFICERS!

LATER... LET'S SEE WHERE WE STAND: ON THE FIRST NIGHT, THEY TRY TO GET RID OF ME... TONIGHT THEY THROW ME A PARTY! UNLESS IT'S A SUBTLE PLOT, WHICH IS POSSIBLE, THEY WOULD HAVE SACRIFICED IGOR...

WHO WOULD ALSO HAVE TO BE QUITE AN ACTOR, SOMETHING I DON'T BELIEVE IS IN HIS NATURE... NO, THEY HAVE ANOTHER GOAL. THEY'RE TRYING TO GET INFORMATION... MERE CURIOSITY OR A SIGN THAT THEY'RE HAVING PROBLEMS?...

DID ANYONE ATTEMPT TO MAKE CONTACT WITH HIM?

NO, NO ONE! HE MUST BE SLEEPING...

WHAT PROBLEMS? AFTER ALL, IT TOOK US 20 YEARS TO PERFECT OUR CARRIER-BORNE AVIATION! I HAVE TO FOCUS ON THAT POINT AND MAKE SURE I DON'T SAY TOO MUCH...

AS FOR THE REST, I SHOULD MOSTLY BE ABLE TO TRUST THEM... ALSO, I'M CURIOUS TO HEAR THE ADMIRAL'S EXPLANATIONS FOR THE OTHER NIGHT'S AMBUSH!

AT DAWN, FURTHER SOUTH...

SO, STILL NOTHING?

NO, SONNY, NOTHING! I'LL TAKE IT AS A GOOD SIGN. BUCK IS ONLY SUPPOSED TO CONTACT US IF HE IS IN TROUBLE...

IT'S STILL BEEN OVER 40 HOURS SINCE WE HEARD ANY NEWS OF HIM... SINCE HE LEFT MOSCOW TO GET ONTO THEIR TUB!

WE'RE SAILING TOWARDS HIM. IVAN HAS DETECTED US ANYWAY, AND THEY'D BE SURPRISED IF WE DIDN'T GO TAKE A CLOSER LOOK AT THEIR "TUB"!

THERE WERE THOSE TWO DOGFIGHTS OUR SATELLITES DETECTED NOT FAR FROM THE ROUTE BUCK MUST HAVE FOLLOWED... AND THE TIMING IS RIGHT TOO!

YOU THINK BUCK COULD HAVE BEEN INVOLVED IN THEM?... THE RUSSIANS WOULD ALREADY HAVE NOTIFIED WASHINGTON!

DAMNED IVAN! YOU ACTUALLY TRUST THEM?!... I'M GOING TO GET SOME FRESH AIR!

BUCK IN THE HANDS OF THE RUSSKIES! HE SHOULD NEVER HAVE ACCEPTED... WE SHOULD HAVE FORBIDDEN HIM FROM DOING SO! IF SOMETHING HAPPENED TO HIM, I'LL NEVER FORGIVE MYSELF!

IN A FEW HOURS WE'LL KNOW... WAITING IS THE HARDEST PART!... WHAT...?!

WHAT'S THAT OVER THERE?... DOLPHINS?... NO, THEY'D BE JUMPING...

IT LOOKS MORE LIKE A... A... PERISCOPE!

ALERT! SUBMARINE ALERT! ALERT! DARN IT! ARE THEY DEAF OR SOMETHING?!

WHAT'S ALL THAT SCREAMING ABOUT?

IT'S ONE OF THE PILOTS FROM THE "TEDDY," SIR!

SUBMARINE!... THEY'LL NEVER HEAR ME... BETTER JUST GO THERE!

MAKE WAY, SAILORS! MAKE WAY!

WOWOWOWOWOW!

ALERT! SUBMARINE AFT OF US!

CAN YOU BELIEVE THIS CLOWN IS AN OFFICER IN THE NAVY?

ACTUALLY, HE'S ON LOAN FROM THE AIR FORCE, SIR!

AH, RIGHT...

I'LL LET YOU KNOW, SIR, THAT YOU ARE ONBOARD ONE OF THE MOST MODERN ANTI-SUBMARINE DESTROYERS! WHAT DO YOU THINK WE USE OUR SONAR FOR? LISTENING TO THE FISH? I KNOW DARNED WELL THAT THERE'S A SUBMARINE!

IT'S BEEN TAILING US SINCE WE ARRIVED IN THE BLACK SEA! I KNOW FLYBOYS HAVE NOTHING BUT DISDAIN FOR DESTROYERS, BUT THAT'S NO REASON TO SPLATTER MY DECK! GET OUT OF MY SIGHT BEFORE I ORDER YOU TO CLEAN IT YOURSELF!

HALF AN HOUR LATER...

ALL THOSE COMMANDERS ARE UNBEARABLE! YOU'D THINK ALL THEIR GOLD LEAVES MAKE THEIR HEADS SWELL UP... THEIR COMPANY IS DOING ME NO GOOD!

FORGIVE ME, GUYS! I'M REALLY SORRY, I...

OH, IT'S ALL RIGHT, SIR, YOU GAVE US A GOOD LAUGH! BUT HURRY ALONG; I'M AFRAID YOU MIGHT STAIN YOUR NICE UNIFORM!

AH, THE COMMENDABLE COURTESY OF THE HARD-WORKING AND EVER-KIND SIMPLE SAILOR! SUCH A COMFORT!

WRROO OAMM

HEY, GUYS! WHAT ARE YOU DOING?

WE'RE TUNING UP THE ENGINE. MY BUDDY CHAVEZ IS LEADING THE 6TH FLEET CHAMPIONSHIP... IT'S THE PRIDE OF THE SHIP!

GOOD-LOOKING MACHINE! CAN I SIT DOWN?

YEAH, BUT DON'T TOUCH ANYTHING, PL...

WATCH IT!

NOOO!

TTTWRRV

HAAAAAAAAAAAAAAAAAAAAAAAAAAH!!!

WRROOHA

DD-971

MAN OVERBOARD!

COME ABOUT 180 DEGREES IMMEDIATELY! WHO IS IT? WHAT HAPPENED?

ER... I THINK IT'S CAPTAIN TUCKSON, SIR... WITH CHAVEZ'S KART!

CHAVEZ'S K... BUT THEN... THE CHAMPIONSHIP IS SCREWED?!

!

Francis Bergese

HA! HA! HA! LOOK AT THIS GUY'S FACE!

THAT'LL TEACH THEM TO COME PLAY TOURISTS IN THE BLACK SEA!

WE'LL FISH HIM OUT... LET IT BE A LESSON TO THEM!

INDEED, IT TAKES THE DESTROYER SEVERAL MINUTES TO COMPLETE ITS MANOEUVRE, WHICH THE RUSSIAN SUB PUTS TO GOOD USE...

WE'LL THROW YOU A LIFEBUOY!

NO, THANKS!

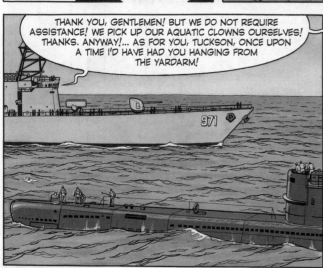

THANK YOU, GENTLEMEN! BUT WE DO NOT REQUIRE ASSISTANCE! WE PICK UP OUR AQUATIC CLOWNS OURSELVES! THANKS. ANYWAY!... AS FOR YOU, TUCKSON, ONCE UPON A TIME I'D HAVE HAD YOU HANGING FROM THE YARDARM!

971

IF I HAD FREE REIN, I WOULD LEAVE YOU WHERE YOU ARE! BUT I JUST RECEIVED THE ORDER TO GET YOU AIRBORNE FOR A RECONNAISSANCE FLIGHT!

YOU OK?

FINE! BUT I SWEAR I'LL NEVER ADD SALT TO MY BACON AND EGGS ANYMORE! URRK!

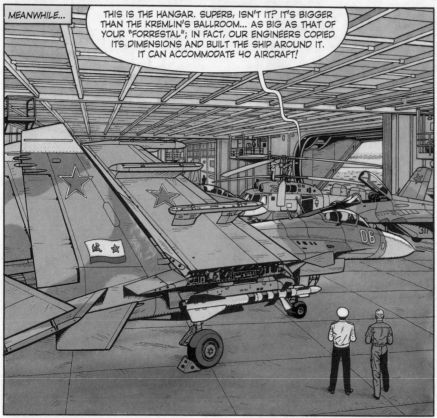

MEANWHILE...

THIS IS THE HANGAR. SUPERB, ISN'T IT? IT'S BIGGER THAN THE KREMLIN'S BALLROOM... AS BIG AS THAT OF YOUR "FORRESTAL"; IN FACT, OUR ENGINEERS COPIED ITS DIMENSIONS AND BUILT THE SHIP AROUND IT. IT CAN ACCOMMODATE 40 AIRCRAFT!

FORTY? YOU'RE STILL FAR FROM THE MARK!

WE'RE JUST STARTING, BUCK! RIGHT NOW WE ONLY HAVE NINE PILOTS QUALIFIED FOR DECK LANDINGS...

THERE'S ALSO A PLANE PROBLEM... WE HAD TO REJECT THE MIG-29 AND THE SU-25... THE FUNDING FOR THE DEVELOPMENT OF AN ADVANCED DETECTION PLANE AND FOR THE YAK-141, AN INCREDIBLE SUPERSONIC VTOL(*), WAS CUT. FORTUNATELY, WE STILL HAVE THE SU-27...

(*)Vertical Take Off and Landing aircraft

FROM WHAT I SAW OF THE SU-27 THE OTHER NIGHT, YOU DON'T HAVE TOO MUCH TO COMPLAIN ABOUT! AND WHAT ABOUT THIS ONE I'M NOT SUPPOSED TO SEE?...

WE HAVE NOTHING TO HIDE FROM YOU, BUCK! NOT EVEN THIS ONE! GIVE ME A HAND!

GOOD LORD! A "TOMCAT"!

YEP! WE HAVE OUR "AGGRESSORS"(*) TOO!

(*)See The Aggressors.

FORMERLY IRANIAN(*), I ASSUME!?

PRECISELY. IT WAS SOLD TO US; AND IF I HEARD RIGHT, FOR A FABULOUS SUM!

(*)Between 1976 and 1978, the Imperial Iranian Air Force bought a total of 80 F-14s. In 1979, the fall of the regime totally changed the country's political situation.

WE GOT HERE JUST IN TIME TO SEE THE TAKE-OFFS. TODAY WE'LL PUT PRACTICALLY EVERYONE IN THE AIR IN YOUR HONOUR!

AS YOU CAN SEE, WE HAVE NO CATAPULTS... OUR BRILLIANT ENGINEERS HAVEN'T MANAGED TO PERFECT THEM YET! A PROBLEM THAT'LL BE SOLVED IN TIME FOR THE NEXT CARRIERS. AT LEAST, I HOPE SO!

IN THE MEANTIME, WE'RE ACQUIRING EXPERIENCE AND TRAINING PILOTS. THE RAMP AND THE CANARD(*) ALLOW US TO LAUNCH AIRCRAFT FROM THE FORWARD SPOTS.

(*)Name given to the airframe configuration in which small stabilising wings are placed forward of the main wings. It doesn't exist on the Su-27s of the Air Force.

BUT THE CANARD MUST COST YOUR SU-27S SPEED AND MANOEUVRABILITY!

AH! YOU'RE TOO SMART, MY FRIEND! IT'S TRUE. WHICH IS WHY WE'RE WORKING ON MAKING THESE SMALL WINGS RETRACTABLE JUST AFTER TAKE-OFF.

AS YOU CAN SEE, THE "KUZNETSOV" IS AN EXPERIMENTAL VESSEL... FAR FROM BEING THE EQUAL OF ONE OF YOUR CARRIERS. THIS IS THE MESSAGE WE WANT TO SEND TO YOUR NAVY, DIRECTLY THROUGH YOU.

YOU MUST UNDERSTAND THAT WE DO NOT HAVE ANY INTENTION TO FIGHT YOU... OUR ENEMIES, AND YOURS, THE REAL ONES, ARE ELSEWHERE!

AH! HERE'S OUR LOCAL TUMBLER! WE THOUGHT YOU MIGHT LIKE TO HAVE A TASTE OF THE "CLUNKER"—OUR OLD VTOL FIGHTER THE YAK-38. I'LL LEAVE YOU NOW; I HAVE TO SEE THE ADMIRAL. MAYBE HE'S RECEIVED SOME NEW DATA?

AT THAT MOMENT, ONBOARD THE AMERICAN DESTROYER...

OK, ROVER, PERMISSION TO TAKE OFF GRANTED! AND IF YOU GET A CHANCE TO DUMP TUCKSON SOMEWHERE ALONG THE WAY, DON'T HESITATE!

ROGER. SONNY, ARE YOU SURE YOU'RE ALL RIGHT?...

DON'T WORRY... EVERYTHING'S FINE! AND ANYTHING RATHER THAN STAY ABOARD THIS TIN CAN!

YOU HAVE TO UNDERSTAND THE CREW'S FURY, SONNY... THEIR KARTING CHAMPIONSHIP CHANCES GOT SUNK!

YEAH... IS THIS WHERE I'M SUPPOSED TO LAUGH? JUST THINK OF BUCK AND FOCUS ON THE MISSION!

SHORTLY AFTERWARDS, ON THE "KUZNETSOV"...

YOU'RE NOT TAKING OFF VERTICALLY?

NO, COLONEL. WE AVOID IT AS MUCH AS POSSIBLE. IT BURNS UP TOO MUCH FUEL, AND THE RANGE SUFFERS. FURTHERMORE, IN VERTICAL MODE THE "CLUNKER" IS EQUIPPED WITH AN AUTOMATIC EJECTION SYSTEM THAT SOMETIMES GOES OFF WITHOUT WARNING... IT'S THE PILOTS' WORST FEAR.

PUMA 2, PUMA 1. CLIMBING TO 3000 FEET, HEADING 035. OVER.

PUMA 2, ACKNOWLEDGED.

NOT FAR FROM THERE...

I HAVE AN ECHO BEARING 126, DISTANCE 20 MILES... IT'S PROBABLY THE "KUZNETSOV"...

IF BUCK IS ABOARD, HE MIGHT SEE US. THAT'LL LIFT HIS SPIRITS... HE PROBABLY NEEDS IT!

OK, LET'S GO. HEADING 126...

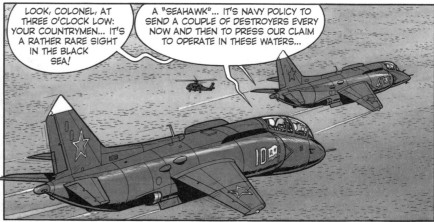

LOOK, COLONEL, AT THREE O'CLOCK LOW: YOUR COUNTRYMEN... IT'S A RATHER RARE SIGHT IN THE BLACK SEA!

A "SEAHAWK"... IT'S NAVY POLICY TO SEND A COUPLE OF DESTROYERS EVERY NOW AND THEN TO PRESS OUR CLAIM TO OPERATE IN THESE WATERS...

HABITS OF THE COLD WAR. HA! HA! INCORRIGIBLE IMPERIALISTS!

I HAVE IT... THERE!... BUT IT'S NOT THE "KUZNETSOV"... WHAT A STRANGE BOAT... NEVER SEEN THE LIKE!

IT'S PAINTED LIKE A MERCHANT SHIP, BUT WITH A GUN TURRET IN THE BOW, A MASSIVE RADOME AND A HELICOPTER PAD AFT...

IT MUST BE ONE OF THEIR EXPERIMENTAL SHIPS... LET'S BE CAREFUL—NO PROVOCATION. KEEP YOUR DISTANCE... I'M CALLING THE DESTROYER TO GET A NEW COURSE TO THE "KUZNETSOV."

NO ANSWER... STRANGE! AND THERE'S SO MUCH FADING!... IT'S AS IF OUR FREQUENCY WAS BEING JAMMED!

PUMA 1, PUMA 2: I HAVE A PROBLEM... MY FUEL LEVEL IS DROPPING ABNORMALLY!

I'VE ONLY GOT 20 MINUTES LEFT...

PUMA 2, PUMA 1. I'LL MAKE A PASS BEHIND YOU TO CHECK THINGS OUT. GOOD OLD "CLUNKER"!

I CAN SEE A TRAIL COMING OUT OF THE FUEL DUMPING SYSTEM... YOU DIDN'T TRIGGER IT BY ANY CHANCE?... THERE, IT STOPPED. HOW MUCH DO YOU HAVE LEFT?

BARELY 10 MINUTES.

I SWEAR, PIOTR, I DIDN'T...

DON'T SWEAT IT, BUDDY! IT WENT OFF BY ITSELF... WE'VE SEEN IT HAPPEN BEFORE! AT ANY RATE, YOU DON'T HAVE ENOUGH FUEL TO GET BACK HOME.

I HAVE AN IDEA, PIOTR... DO YOU REMEMBER THAT KGB* BOAT ON WHICH WE LANDED THE "CLUNKERS" LAST YEAR?! IT MUST BE CLOSE BY...

RIGHT. I'M CALLING THEM... THEIR CALL SIGN IS "COBRA"...

(*)All-powerful political police and intelligence service of the USSR

SOON...

WE'RE ALMOST THERE. MAKING THE APPROACH ON MINIMUM ENGINE POWER, I'LL HAVE ENOUGH FUEL TO ATTEMPT VERTICAL LANDING.

GO AHEAD, BUDDY... AND REMEMBER THAT THE "CLUNKER" HANDLES LIKE AN ANVIL!

30A

AT LAST...

GREAT JOB, TUMBLER! FLAWLESS! SUPERB!

?... WHAT THE... ALERT! AAAH!

Francis Bergèse

30B

WE'VE SEEN ENOUGH. LET'S GO HOME!

NO, WAIT! THE SECOND "FORGER"(*) WAS JUST SHOT DOWN!

(*)Codename given by NATO forces to the Yak-38. The Su-27 is called "Flanker."

STEP ON IT, DRIVER! WE'RE GONNA GET A CLOSER LOOK!

BUT SONNY... YOU THINK THAT...

GO! MY INTUITION IS TELLING ME WE ABSOLUTELY HAVE TO GO!

GET OUT, COLONEL! THIS IS WHERE OUR PATHS MUST DIVERGE... THEY SHOULD NEVER EVEN HAVE CROSSED!

!

DON'T WORRY, CAPTAIN STORNIK. NO MESSAGES HAVE BEEN TRANSMITTED... WE'RE JAMMING ALL FREQUENCIES.

VERY GOOD! STOP THE JAMMING NOW.

NOW THIS IS GETTING SERIOUS!... UNFRIENDLY OR HOSTILE IVAN, FINE! BUT I DON'T LIKE THE LOOK OF THESE MARTIANS!

IT'S TIME TO USE MY DISTRESS BEACON... I HAVE TO GET AWAY FROM THEM, IF ONLY FOR A MOMENT OR TWO...

MPFF...

HE'S GETTING AWAY! DON'T SHOOT! I WANT HIM ALIVE! LAUNCH A BOAT, QUICK!

REVERSE ENGINES FULL!

WHO'S THE MORON IN CHARGE OF THIS DETAIL?!

ER... I AM, CAPTAIN... JUNIOR LIEUTENANT PLATYPOV!

... PRESS THE BUTTON AND COME UP FURTHER AWAY...

WAS THIS RIDICULOUS IDEA OF NBC(*) COMBINATIONS YOURS, PLATYPOV?

ER... YES, CAPTAIN. THE KGB MANUAL INSISTS ON THE PSYCHOLOGICAL EFFECT OF THESE SUITS... THEY'RE SUPPOSED TO IMPRESS PRISONERS!

(*)Nuclear, Bacteriological, Chemical

YOU COMPLETE FOOL! YOU DO NOT HAVE A SPY OF THIS CALIBRE GUARDED BY COSMONAUTS!

FASTER, TUMB! THEY'VE PUT A BOAT TO SEA!

I'M AT TOP SPEED!

THERE HE IS! I WONDER WHAT HE WAS HOPING TO ACCOMPLISH. THE COAST IS ALMOST 60 MILES AWAY!

HEY! LOOK AT WHAT'S COMING THERE!

WHAT IS THAT HELICOPTER DOING HERE?! AN AMERICAN ONE ON TOP OF THAT! BRING IT DOWN AT ALL COSTS! SHOOT DOWN THOSE IMPERIALISTS!

THEY'VE JUST FISHED SOMEONE OUT OF THE DRINK... GOOD LORD! IT'S BUCK!

ARE YOU SURE?

SURE AS I CAN SEE YOU AND THE GUYS SHOOTING AT US!

DON'T LET THEM GET AWAY! FIRE! **FIRE!**

HELL! SAMS(*)! LAUNCH FLARES, QUICK!

BEEEP BEEEP BEEE

(*)Surface-to-Air Missile

33A

PHEW! THAT WAS DAMN CLOSE!... SO YOU SAW BUCK?... ARE YOU ABSOLUTELY SURE?!

OH, YOU BLOCKHEAD! DO I HAVE TO SING IT TO YOU?! **YES! I'M SUUURE!**

FINE, FINE! BUT IT SEEMS SO INCREDIBLE... INEXPLICABLE!... AND SINCE WE'RE OUT OF RANGE, HOW ABOUT YOU DROP THE FIREWORKS?!

ER... WELL, ALL THE FLARES(*) ARE GONE, ANYWAY!

LET'S GET BACK TO BASE. WE'LL CONTACT WASHINGTON AND RAISE THE ALARM.

(*)Thermal decoys used to lure heat-seeking missiles

MEANWHILE, ABOARD THE "KUZNETSOV"...

I'M IN PRIMARY FLIGHT CONTROL, ADMIRAL... THE LATEST NEWS HAD PUMA 2 ABOUT TO LAND ON THE SPECIAL SHIP "LADOZNSKOYE" WHEN CONTACT WAS LOST DUE TO AN EXTREMELY STRONG PARASITE SIGNAL!

THIS IS VERY SERIOUS, IGOR... I JUST RECEIVED A FAX FROM KOLINKA, OUR LISTENING CENTRE. IT'S ABOUT YOUR ADVENTURES LAST NIGHT... LISTEN...

33B

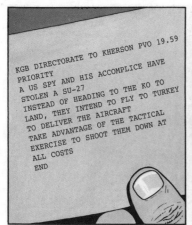

KGB DIRECTORATE TO KHERSON PVO 19.59
PRIORITY
A US SPY AND HIS ACCOMPLICE HAVE
STOLEN A SU-27
INSTEAD OF HEADING TO THE KO TO
LAND, THEY INTEND TO FLY TO TURKEY
TO DELIVER THE AIRCRAFT
TAKE ADVANTAGE OF THE TACTICAL
EXERCISE TO SHOOT THEM DOWN AT
ALL COSTS
END

KOLINKA ADDS: "IT IS INEXPLICABLE THAT SUCH A MESSAGE WASN'T TRANSMITTED OVER THE PVO'S GENERAL NETWORK BUT ONLY TO THE KHERSON BASE DIRECTLY..."

THE KGB AND THE PVO ACTING WITHOUT ORDERS FROM THE GOVERNMENT! THIS SOUNDS LIKE A CONSPIRACY!...

PRECISELY... A CONSPIRACY OF WHICH BUCK DANNY WOULD BE BOTH TARGET AND CRUX!

AND THIS NEW INCIDENT WITH THE RADIO JAMMING. STRANGE!

WAIT, ADMIRAL... WE'RE RECEIVING A NEW MESSAGE!

GREAT GODS! IT'S FROM THE "LADOZNSKOYE": "16.04... COLLISION BETWEEN PUMA 1 AND 2... LOW PROBABILITY OF SURVIVORS... PROCEEDING WITH SEARCH ANYWAY..." THIS IS HORRIBLE!

THE POOR MAN... WE'RE RESPONSIBLE FOR THIS TRAGEDY! AND IF ONLY IT WAS JUST ABOUT US... BUT THE CONSEQUENCES, IGOR...

THE CONSEQUENCES... OUR RELATIONS WITH THE UNITED STATES DAMAGED... AND HERE, THIS PROBABLE PLOT DIVIDING OUR ARMED FORCES!

EXACTLY, ADMIRAL; WE NEED TO BE CERTAIN! I'M TAKING THE SHUTTLE HELICOPTER AND HEADING TO THE "LADOZNSKOYE." HAVE A PAIR OF "CLUNKERS" ARMED WITH GUN AND ROCKET PODS READY!

WE MUST BE PREPARED TO FACE ANY NEW CRISIS!

ALL RIGHT. BUT TAKE A FEW ARMED MEN AS AN ESCORT... WE'LL FOLLOW YOU... I'M ORDERING A NEW COURSE TOWARDS THE "LADOZNSKOYE"...

ANOTHER THING, IGOR... STRICTLY BETWEEN US... I FEEL OVERWHELMED BY ALL THIS, OUT OF MY DEPTH... SUDDENLY I'M A VERY OLD MAN...

... I CAN SEE WHAT'S COMING... NOTHING IN MY LIFE OR CAREER HAS PREPARED ME FOR IT. THEREFORE, I'VE MADE A DECISION: YOU'RE TAKING EFFECTIVE OPERATIONAL COMMAND. I'M KEEPING NOMINAL COMMAND: YOU DECIDE, I'LL TAKE RESPONSIBILITY...

MEANWHILE, TUMBLER AND SONNY HAVE RETURNED TO THE "DAVID W. RAY," THEIR DESTROYER...

YOU'RE TAKING OFF AGAIN AS SOON AS YOU'RE REFUELLED! A FLEETSATCOM MESSAGE JUST ARRIVED: YOUR FRIEND TURNED HIS BEACON ON... HERE'S HIS POSITION!

WE KNOW IT... WE SAW HIM! TAKE CARE OF THE REFUELLING, LIEUTENANT. WE'RE GOING TO REPORT TO THE SKIPPER(*)!

(*)The ship's captain, in sailor slang

A FEW MINUTES LATER, THE TWO PILOTS ARE WRAPPING UP THEIR REPORT...

ARE YOU SURE?... SO COLONEL DANNY IS IVAN'S PRISONER! WE SHOULD NEVER HAVE TRUSTED THEM!

WE'LL WORRY ABOUT THE "KUZNETSOV" LATER... FIRST, LET'S TAKE CARE OF THIS PIRATE! HE'S GOING TO LEARN THE PRICE OF DEFYING THE UNITED STATES!

WE'RE NOT LETTING HIM OUT OF OUR SIGHT! ROD, CHART THE NEW ROUTE AND WARN WASHINGTON! IT'S ON!

AYE, AYE, SIR!

35A

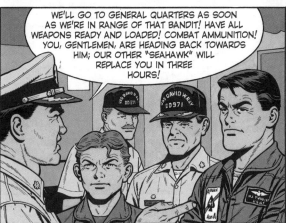

WE'LL GO TO GENERAL QUARTERS AS SOON AS WE'RE IN RANGE OF THAT BANDIT! HAVE ALL WEAPONS READY AND LOADED! COMBAT AMMUNITION! YOU, GENTLEMEN, ARE HEADING BACK TOWARDS HIM; OUR OTHER "SEAHAWK" WILL REPLACE YOU IN THREE HOURS!

SIR, MAY I REMIND YOU THAT OUR "SEAHAWK" IS AN EXPERIMENTAL VERSION, AND THAT ITS EQUIPMENT IS MORE POWERFUL THAN YOUR EMBARKED HELO? ALLOW US TO OPERATE ALONE, WITH EXTRA FUEL TANKS!

SIR, I SECOND MAJOR TUMBLER'S REQUEST! BUCK IS OUR FRIEND... IF NEED BE, WE'D RATHER RETURN TO REFUEL QUICKLY AND GO BACK OURSELVES!

VERY WELL, GENTLEMEN... I ACCEPT YOUR ARGUMENTS! YOUR CALL SIGN WILL BE... LET'S SEE... "RESCUE"! AS FOR MINE, THAT REQUIRES REFLECTION... ER... "TORGAU"(*)... THAT'S IT, "TORGAU"! IF I'M TO BE THE ONE WHO MIGHT FIRE THE OPENING SHOTS OF WORLD WAR THREE, THAT OUGHT TO GIVE THEM PAUSE...

(*)Small German town on the Elbe River where Americans and Soviets met on April 25, 1945

35B

A FEW MINUTES LATER...

GLAD TO BE HEADING BACK OUT, EH, TUMBLER?... I MUST ADMIT THE SKIPPER AMAZED ME! HE SEEMS DETERMINED TO SINK THEIR BUCKET IF HE HAS TO! I HOPE HE'S NOT FORGETTING THAT BUCK'S ONBOARD!

THIS COMMANDER CODY IS SMARTER THAN HE SEEMS. IF IVAN INTERCEPTS OUR MESSAGES, WHICH IS UNAVOIDABLE, HE'S SENDING THEM A SIGNAL... OUR RADIO CALL SIGNS, THE WORD "RESCUE" AND THE NAME OF A PLACE WHERE OUR TROOPS AND THEIRS FRATERNISED, SHOULD MAKE THEM UNDERSTAND OUR INTENTIONS: WE ARE DETERMINED BUT AREN'T COMING AS ENEMIES!

CLEVER!

LATER...

I HAVE IT, TUMB! STRAIGHT AHEAD AT 19 NAUTICAL MILES... OH?... I HAVE ANOTHER ECHO... THERE'S A HELICOPTER CIRCLING IT!

CAPTAIN STORNIK! FOR THE LAST TIME, I REPEAT THAT I HAVE EVERY INTENT TO LAND ON YOUR SHIP AND CONDUCT A SEARCH!

CAPTAIN ALEXENKO! LET ME REPEAT FOR THE LAST TIME THAT I AM ON AN ULTRA-CONFIDENTIAL AND HIGHLY IMPORTANT MISSION FOR THE KGB... THIS IS WHY WE JAMMED COMMUNICATIONS... WE STOPPED RIGHT AFTER YOUR PLANES COLLIDED!

... I AM UNDER STRICT ORDERS NOT TO LET ANYONE ONBOARD! IF YOU DO NOT STAY CLEAR, I WILL GIVE THE ORDER TO OPEN FIRE! THIS IS MY LAST WARNING!

SO YOU ADMIT THE JAMMING!... IT STARTED AT THE TIME OF PUMA 1'S FINAL APPROACH TO YOUR LANDING PAD! YOUR VERSION DOESN'T ADD UP!

I WARN YOU, ALEXENKO!

YOU WIN FOR THE MOMENT... BUT WE'LL BE BACK! AND IT IS YOU, STORNIK, WHO SHALL BEAR FULL RESPONSIBILITY FOR WHAT WILL HAPPEN!

GOOD RIDDANCE, ALEXENKO!

SHUT THIS RADIO OFF! THEY WON'T GET OFF OUR BACK... WE HAVE TO BUY SOME TIME... REMOVE THE EVIDENCE; GET RID OF THE AMERICAN AND YOUR PLANE, TUMBLER... AS SOON AS THIS MORON IS OUT OF SIGHT, HAVE IT DUMPED OVERBOARD!

"KUZNETSOV," "KUZNETSOV," THIS IS CAPTAIN ALEXENKO... I NEED TO SPEAK TO THE ADMIRAL!

I'M LISTENING, IGOR... I WAS ON THE BRIDGE.

GET THE "CLUNKERS" IN THE AIR IMMEDIATELY IF THEY'RE READY. HAVE THEM FIRE WARNING SHOTS ACROSS THE BOW OF THE "LADOZNSKOYE" AND ORDER IT TO STOP...

... THEN, IF THE ORDER HASN'T BEEN OBEYED AFTER THREE MINUTES, HAVE THEM FIRE THEIR ROCKETS INTO ITS STERN... THAT'LL STOP IT!

IGOR, ARE YOU SURE YOU KNOW WHAT YOU'RE DOING?

POSITIVE! ON OUR WAY TO THE "LADOZNSKOYE," WE SAW AN AMERICAN DESTROYER LITERALLY FLYING TOWARDS IT... THE YANKEES MUST BE ON TO SOMETHING... WE MUST GET IN CONTACT WITH THEM, LEARN WHAT THEY KNOW AND CONVINCE THEM NOT TO ACT!

YOU'RE RIGHT! WE DON'T NEED ANOTHER INTERNATIONAL INCIDENT!

LYNX 1 AND 2, IMMEDIATE TAKE-OFF! HERE ARE THE DETAILS OF YOUR MISSION...

MOMENTS LATER...

FORCE A KGB SHIP TO HEAVE TO... NOW, THAT'S A NEW ONE!

YEAH! MUST BE A HELL OF A FIX HIGHER UP!

AT THE SAME TIME...

WHAT A MESS, TUMB! TO THINK THAT BUCK IS JUST OVER THERE, A PRISONER, MAYBE BEING TORTURED BY THOSE SAVAGES!... AND ALL WE HAVE IS OUR SIDE ARMS! HEY, WAIT... THEY'RE PUSHING THE "FORGER" OVERBOARD!

EVERYTHING IS STRANGE, TODAY! I WONDER WHAT WAS THE MEANING OF THAT KAMOV'S ANTICS... IN ANY CASE, IT LEFT WITHOUT LANDING!

LOOK AT THE RADIO! THE JAMMING LIGHT IS BLINKING... OH? IT JUST TURNED OFF! I'M CALLING CODY...

TORGAU, RESCUE... TORGAU, RESCUE, DO YOU READ ME?

TORGAU HERE, WE READ YOU FIVE BY FIVE. WE FOUND A ROTATING FREQUENCY ALGORITHM THEY CAN'T KEEP UP WITH! I KNEW WE'D BE THE BEST AT THIS LITTLE GAME!

THIS IS RESCUE. SOMETHING'S HAPPENING HERE! I HAVE TWO ECHOES ON A FAST APPROACH!

KO, LYNX 1, WE HAVE THE "LADOZNSKOYE" IN SIGHT! I MUST REPORT THE PRESENCE OF A NON-SOVIET HELICOPTER NEARBY... REQUESTING CONFIRMATION OF OUR ORDERS!

THIS IS CAPTAIN ALEXENKO! I'M CONFIRMING THE ORDERS IN ADMIRAL FRONDZE'S NAME! EXECUTE!

LYNX 1 TO "LADOZNSKOYE," I'M UNDER STRICT ORDERS TO BRING YOU TO A HALT. STOP YOUR ENGINES... IMMEDIATELY!

IF YOU DO NOT COMPLY, WE WILL OPEN FIRE!

ACKNOWLEDGED, LYNX 1... AND NOW LISTEN TO MY ORDERS TO THE CREW: BATTLE STATIONS! RAISE THE COLOURS!

YOU WON'T BE CRAZY ENOUGH TO ATTACK A KGB SHIP IN THE COURSE OF ITS DUTY!

WE'LL SEE ABOUT THAT!

YOU WILL ANSWER FOR IT WITH YOUR LIVES, AND THOSE OF YOUR FAMILIES! I HAVE WARNED YOU! IT'S NOT TOO LATE!

TATATATATATATATAT

LYNX 1 HERE: THIS WAS OUR LAST WARNING, "LADOZNSKOYE"!

I'M NOT STOPPING, GENTLEMEN! WHAT ARE YOU GOING TO DO NOW?!

FOLLOW MY ORDERS! FOR YOUR INFORMATION, KNOW THAT MY FATHER IS SAFE FROM YOUR RETALIATION: HE WAS ALREADY EXECUTED BY THE KGB IN 1968!

NIKOLAI... I THINK THIS IS MADNESS!

39A

LYNX 2, THIS IS CAPTAIN STORNIK! DO NOT FOLLOW THIS TRAITOR AND SON OF A TRAITOR!

FORGIVE ME, NIKOLAI... I CAN'T!

DO AS YOUR CONSCIENCE DICTATES, JOSEF... BUT I'M ATTACKING!

NAVY

TORGAU? STILL THERE?... THIS IS UNBELIEVABLE! THE "FORGERS" JUST FIRED WHAT LOOKED LIKE A WARNING SHOT... THEN THEY SPLIT UP, AND IT LOOKS LIKE THE LEADER IS PREPARING FOR AN ATTACK RUN! THE SHIP IS TURNING NOW...

39B

HELL! HE'S TURNING TIGHT! AND I'M NOT CLOSE ENOUGH TO FIRE MY ROCKETS WITH ANY KIND OF ACCURACY...

THE ORDERS ARE CLEAR: I'M ONLY SUPPOSED TO HIT THE PROPELLERS AND RUDDER TO IMMOBILIZE HIM... TOO LATE! I'LL HAVE TO MAKE ANOTHER PASS...

GUN CREW, FIRE! FIRE!

HE'S BREAKING OFF... PERFECT! MISSILE LAUNCHERS, NOW... FIRE!

BY THE RODINA(*)!... NIKOLAI DIDN'T FIRE AND THEY SHOT HIM DOWN WITHOUT BATTING AN EYELASH! BASTARDS! KO, KO, LYNX 2... THEY... THEY GOT LYNX 1! I'M GOING IN!

(*)Motherland

HARD TO STARBOARD! NOW!

SHARP TURN... DON'T GIVE THEM TIME TO DO THE SAME...

OH, RATS, HE'S GOING TO...

HE'S FIRING! **HIT THE DECK!**

BADOOM BWAHM

BRIDGE, THIS IS THE ENGINE ROOM! NO RESPONSE FROM THE RUDDER OR THE PROPELLERS! WE'RE STOPPED!

TRAITORS, ALL OF THEM! THEY LEAVE ME NO CHOICE... WE'RE LAUNCHING OPERATION "RED LIGHTNING." YOU KNOW THE DRILL... AND ABOVE ALL, WARN MOSCOW!

NIGHT'S COMING IN TWO HOURS... IT'LL DO!

PERFECT! HAVE THE AMERICAN SPY BROUGHT TO MY QUARTERS. I WANT TO SPEAK TO HIM!

TORGAU, RESCUE. I SAY AGAIN: THE PIRATE IS DEAD IN THE WATER! IT'S CLEAR THAT NAVAL AVIATION ISN'T ON HIS SIDE! I FIGURE, IF THEY WANTED TO COME TO BUCK'S AID, THAT'S EXACTLY HOW THEY'D GO ABOUT IT. WHAT DO YOU THINK?

HMM... YOU MAY BE RIGHT... THEIR ADMIRAL'S BEEN CALLING ME OVER EVERY POSSIBLE FREQUENCY FOR SOME TIME! COULD HE MEAN IT? IS THIS A RISK WORTH TAKING? I'M GOING TO ANSWER HIM. STAY ON THE LINE!

ABOARD THE "LADOZNSKOYE"...

OH!... MY HEAD FEELS HEAVY!... I BET THEY DRUGGED ME...

FOLLOW ME; THE CAPTAIN WANTS TO SEE YOU.

I'D BETTER CLEAR MY HEAD REAL SOON... OH? THE SHIP HAS STOPPED?!

AH! HERE'S OUR AMERICAN SPY! JUDGING BY THE EFFORTS MADE TO GET YOU BACK, YOU MUST BE DAMNED IMPORTANT! LEAVE US, PLATYPOV. TUMBLER AND I ARE BIG ENOUGH TO KEEP AN EYE ON HIM!

THERE'S AN OLD RUSSIAN SAYING: "NO MAN SHOULD DIE WITHOUT KNOWING WHY..." CAPTAIN TUMBLER, IS EVERYTHING READY?

YES, CAPTAIN. OPERATION RED LIGHTNING HAS BEGUN!

GOOD! YOU SEE, MR EVANS... OR RATHER, COLONEL DANNY, WHEN WE HEARD ABOUT THE INVITATION THE BLACK SEA FLEET HAD EXTENDED TO YOU, WE WERE SHOCKED... COULD THEY BE THAT STUPID?!

WE QUICKLY GRASPED THE INCREDIBLE CHANCE THAT THIS INSANE INITIATIVE OFFERED US! OUR COUNTRY IS ON THE VERGE OF COLLAPSE, OUR PEOPLE ARE DISCOURAGED, DIVIDED... THEY'VE LOST FAITH IN OUR REVOLUTION. POWER IS IN FECKLESS OR TRAITOROUS HANDS!

WE MUST ELIMINATE THOSE IMPOSTORS... BUT WITHOUT ADDING TO THE DIVISIONS AMONG THE PEOPLE AND WHILE REKINDLING THEIR COURAGE. AND SO IT SHALL BE, **THANKS TO YOU, COLONEL DANNY!**

IN A FEW HOURS, YOU WILL BE LEADING A COMMANDO OF ASSASSINS ASHORE NEAR THE DACHA WHERE ONE PRESIDENT GORBACHEV IS VACATIONING... YOU WILL MURDER HIM JUST BEFORE YOU ARE YOURSELF SHOT! THIS IS WHAT THE WORLD WILL HEAR. THE SHAME OF SUCH A CRIME WILL REBOUND ONTO YOUR COUNTRY AND YOUR LEADERS!

I'VE NEVER HEARD ANYTHING SO RIDICU-LOUS!... NO ONE WILL BELIEVE YOU! BY LAYING THE BLAME FOR THIS CRIME ON MY COUNTRY, YOU WILL BRING THE WORLD TO THE BRINK OF NUCLEAR WAR!

PRECISELY! AND IN THAT CRUCIBLE, ANGER MIXING WITH FEAR, WE SHALL FORGE THE UNITY OF OUR GREAT PEOPLE ANEW, AGAINST YOU, AND UNDER THE LEADERSHIP OF A RENEWED, PURGED PARTY... WE WILL BE BELIEVED. OUR PROPAGANDA MACHINE IS WELL OILED!

DO YOU FIND MY PISTOL FASCI-NATING, COLONEL?... DON'T TRY ANYTHING, TUMBLER'S GOT GOOD REFLEXES, AND YOUR SUICIDE WOULDN'T STOP YOUR CORPSE FROM REACHING THE BEACH AT FAROS!

I'LL CONFESS SOMETHING TO YOU: THERE ARE A FEW FAINT AT HEART WITHIN OUR MOVEMENT WHO ARE NOT FAR FROM SHAR-ING YOUR OPINION OF OUR PLAN. THEY'RE THE ONES WHO, AS A LAST-DITCH MEASURE, TRIED TO HAVE YOU ELIMINATED BETWEEN MOSCOW AND THE BLACK SEA... WE CONTRIBUTED SOMEWHAT TO THE "KUZNETSOV'S" INTERVENTION BY LETTING AIR DEFENCE'S MESSAGES LEAK FROM ITS SECRET FREQUENCY!

WHY ARE YOU SO DETER-MINED?!

WITHOUT THE PARTY THAT SAVED US, THE NAZIS WOULD HAVE DESTROYED THE ENTIRE RUSSIAN PEOPLE! I AM THE ONLY SURVIVOR OF A FAMILY MASSACRED TO THE LAST PERSON, AND I SWORE TO DEDICATE MY LIFE TO THIS CAUSE!

YOU'RE A DEGENERATE FANATIC! NO ONE WILL FOLLOW YOU! YOU DON'T STAND A CHANCE OF GETTING ME TO THE COAST OF CRIMEA!

WE'LL SEE ABOUT THAT. TAKE HIM AWAY!

AT THAT MOMENT...

THIS WAITING IS KILLING ME... I CAN'T STAND IT ANYMORE! NOT A WORD FROM CODY FOR ALMOST AN HOUR... THE "FORGER" HAS BEEN REPLACED BY A SURVEILLANCE KAMOV. NOTHING'S HAPPENING AND NIGHT IS COMING...

TAKE THE STICK FOR A WHILE—THAT'LL KEEP YOU BUSY!

43A

RESCUE, TORGAU! ARE YOU ASLEEP OR SOMETHING?! 'CAUSE THIS ISN'T THE TIME FOR IT!

YOU ARE TO FLY IMMEDIATELY TO THE "KUZNETSOV," AT 90 NAUTICAL MILES ON HEADING 232, AND LAND THERE. YOU'RE EXPECTED... DO YOU HAVE ENOUGH FUEL?

WE'RE GOOD. BUT, SIR... WHAT IF IT'S A TRAP?

NOT A CHANCE! THEIR ADMIRAL'S CONVINCED ME. THEY'RE GOING TO BOARD THE PIRATE... YOU'LL BE THE LIAI-SON. RESCUE 2 IS ON ITS WAY TO RELIEVE YOU!

BOARD IT!? WITH IVAN'S USUAL BLOODTHIRSTY CARELESSNESS!? THEY'RE INSANE! WHAT ABOUT BUCK?!

I DON'T LIKE IT MUCH EITHER!

RESCUE 1! DO YOU THINK I'M GOING TO RISK STARTING WORLD WAR THREE TO MAKE YOU HAPPY? THIS IS YOUR FRIEND'S ONLY CHANCE!

MEANWHILE...

DANNY'S LOCKED UP AGAIN. THE RADAR REPORTS THAT THEIR HELICOPTERS ARE ROTATING TO WATCH US... NOW, RED LIGHTNING!

43B

ALTHOUGH SCARED, THE MOSCOW COMMITTEE FINALLY GAVE ITS AGREEMENT. IT WASN'T EASY, BUT THEY REALISED THEY DIDN'T HAVE A CHOICE... THEY'RE LAUNCHING THE OPERATION TONIGHT. THE "ORLYONOK" SHOULD BE ABOUT TO TAKE OFF WITH 70 SPETSNAZ(*), WHO WILL LAND AT FAROS WITH DANNY...

(*)Special Forces

THE "ORLYONOK" WILL RENDEZVOUS WITH US 10 MINUTES AFTER SUN-DOWN. DANNY, YOU, ME AND PLATYPOV WILL TRANSFER ABOARD...

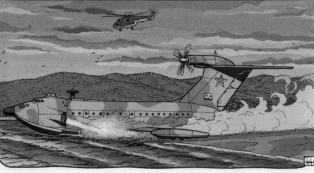

THEN, AT LOW SPEED SO AS TO BLEND IN WITH SURFACE TRAFFIC ON RADARS, WE'LL FOLLOW A WIDE, LOOPING TRAJECTORY THAT WILL PUT US ON FAROS AT DAWN, FROM A DIRECTION OUR PURSUERS CANNOT POSSIBLY EXPECT...

IN ORDER FOR THE PLAN TO SUCCEED, IT IS CRUCIAL THAT THE "ORLYONOK" NOT BE IDENTIFIED, WHICH IMPLIES THAT WE MUST FIRST GET RID OF THE HELICOPTERS KEEPING TABS ON US...

WHICH IS WHY SQUADRON 351 WILL SWEEP THE SKIES CLEAN SIX MINUTES BEFORE THE ORLYONOK'S ARRIVAL. IT'LL BE CLOSE, BUT I'M CONFIDENT!

TOO CLOSE! MOREOVER, I DON'T TRUST PLATYPOV... HE'S JUST A STUPID UKRAINIAN! KEEP HIS ROLE TO A MINIMUM!

I'D LIKE TO BUY MORE TIME... I THINK I HAVE AN IDEA... WE'LL SEND A NEW MESSAGE TO THE "KUZNETSOV"...

A BIT LATER...

"KUZNETSOV," THIS IS RESCUE 1 ON FINAL APPROACH!

LAND IN FRONT OF THE ISLAND, RESCUE 1. WE'VE BEEN EAGERLY WAITING FOR YOU... WELCOME!

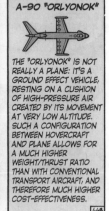

A-90 "ORLYONOK"

THE "ORLYONOK" IS NOT REALLY A PLANE: IT'S A GROUND EFFECT VEHICLE, RESTING ON A CUSHION OF HIGH-PRESSURE AIR CREATED BY ITS MOVEMENT AT VERY LOW ALTITUDE. SUCH A CONFIGURATION BETWEEN HOVERCRAFT AND PLANE ALLOWS FOR A MUCH HIGHER WEIGHT/THRUST RATIO THAN WITH CONVENTIONAL TRANSPORT AIRCRAFT, AND THEREFORE MUCH HIGHER COST-EFFECTIVENESS.

TUMBLER! TUCKSON! I WOULD HAVE MUCH PREFERRED MEETING YOU UNDER DIFFERENT CIRCUMSTANCES! BUT DANNY'S ALIVE; THAT'S THE MAIN THING!

WE'LL DO EVERYTHING WE CAN TO RESCUE HIM. WE'RE PREPARING AN ASSAULT ON THE "LADOZ" WITH HELICOPTERS AND COMMANDOES!

YES, WELL... ACTUALLY, CAPTAIN, YOUR PLAN SOUNDS RISKY TO US!

THERE'S EVERY CHANCE THAT BUCK WILL LOSE HIS LIFE IN THAT SCUFFLE... OUR OPPONENTS HAVE ALREADY SHOWN THAT THEY WILL STOP AT NOTHING!

I KNOW, MY FRIENDS... I KNOW... BUT DO WE REALLY HAVE A CHOICE?... WE HAVE NO IDEA WHAT THEIR INTENTIONS ARE, EXCEPT THAT THEY'RE PART OF A BIGGER PLAN... THEY MUST BE INTENDING TO USE DANNY SOMEHOW, SO IT'S IN THEIR INTEREST TO KEEP HIM ALIVE...

45A

... EVEN IF WE STORM THEIR SHIP!

I THINK YOU'RE AN OPTIMIST!

CAPTAIN ALEXENKO AND THE AMERICAN PILOTS TO REPORT TO THE ADMIRAL IMMEDIATELY!

SOON...

WE HAVE NEWS, GENTLEMEN! THIS MESSAGE FROM THE "LADOZ" TELLS ME THAT PART OF THE CREW MUTINIED. THEY CAPTURED STORNIK AND FREED BUCK, WHO'S SAFE. THEY'RE HOLED UP IN THE CENTRE OF THE SHIP.

WHAT?!

THAT'S BRILLIANT! GOOD LORD! LET'S GO, FOLKS! WE CAN CHARGE IN AND GET BUCK BACK!

I CANNOT STOP YOU FROM DOING SO... BUT YOU SHOULD KNOW THAT THE MUTINEERS ARE BEGGING US TO DO NOTHING...

?

Francis Bergese

45B

THEY'RE WORRIED THEY CAN'T HOLD BACK AN ATTACK FROM STORNIK'S LOYALISTS. BUT, OF COURSE, THIS IS NO CONCERN TO AN AMERICAN HELICOPTER APPROACHING ALONE...

OBVIOUSLY, I CANNOT GUARANTEE WHAT KIND OF WELCOME YOU'LL RECEIVE!... IGOR, YOU CAN GO WITH THEM! JUST IN CASE, I'M SENDING TWO SUKHOIS ON DISTANT COVER.

TERRIBLE TIME WHEN EACH MAN MUST MAKE HIS OWN DECISIONS... NO, I WAS REALLY NOT PREPARED FOR THAT!... GO, YOUNG MEN!

THANK YOU, ADMIRAL!

46A

MEANWHILE...

TORGAU, RESCUE 2. WE'RE ON STATION NEAR THE "LADOZNSKOYE." IT'S SETTLING SLOWLY FROM THE AFT...

WAIT! OUR RADAR DETECTOR SHOWS SOME AIRCRAFT COMING IN FROM THE NORTHEAST!

"LADOZ," THIS IS RED MONSTER. WE'VE JUST PICKED YOU UP ON OUR RADAR... WE'LL BE WITH YOU IN FIVE MINUTES. GET READY!

"LADOZ," THIS IS RED AND GOLD DRAGON, WE HAVE A VISUAL ON YOU. RED 2 AND 4, TAKE CARE OF THE KAMOV; RED 3 WITH ME TO ELIMINATE THE YANKEE.

46B

RED 2 HERE. THANK YOU, COMRADE! WE'RE GOING TO BLOW THIS LITTLE REVISIONIST SAILOR TO SMITHEREENS!

WHAT...? SOME MIGS ARE FIRING MISSILES AT US!

EVADE, ALEXEI! EVADE!

46C

MISSION ACCOMPLISHED. HEADING BACK!

TORGAU, RESCUE 2... THEY...THEY SHOT DOWN THE KAMOV... NEVER HAD A CHANCE!... TWO MORE ARE HEADING FOR US!

FOX FOX FOX!(*) HEAD DOWN! DIVE! IT'S OUR ONLY CHANCE!

(*)Missile alert

47A

JUST HOPE THOSE MISSILES HAVE A MINIMUM ALTITUDE AND THAT WE'RE BELOW IT!

LOWER, JEFF! LOWER!

OUR WHEELS ARE IN THE WATER AND WE COULD DROWN THE TURBINES!

HURRAY! IT WORKED!

MAYBE THE WATER LIFTED BY THE ROTOR CONFUSED THEIR GUIDANCE SYSTEMS!

RESCUE 2, RESCUE 1. HANG ON TIGHT, BOYS! THE SUKHOIS FROM THE "KUZNETSOV" ARE COMING!

47B

LOOK OUT! TWO OF THE MISSILES ARE LOOPING BACK!

?!

UNBELIEVABLE! ONE OF THOSE GOONS JUST GOT SMOKED BY ONE OF HIS OWN MISSILES! BUT THE OTHER ONE'S COMING BACK!

THIS IS ALBATROSS 1. HANG TIGHT, YANKEE BOYS! I'M LINING UP THIS FASCIST!

48A

BUT THAT DOESN'T TAKE INTO ACCOUNT THE MIG-29S OF GOLD DRAGON FLIGHT...

ALERT! HOSTILES AT 3 O'CLOCK!

THEY GOT RED 1!

KEEP YOUR COOL! GOLD 3 WITH ME ON THE LEADER, 2 AND 4 ON THE WINGMAN!

AND USE YOUR GUNS, COMRADES! LET'S NOT GIVE THEM ANY CHANCE TO EVADE OUR MISSILES WITH THEIR FAMOUS "COBRA"!

AARGH!

48B

AND SO THE MIGS CAN FINISH THEIR DIRTY WORK...

RESCUE 2 HERE... THIS TIME IT'S OVER... GOODBYE, FOLKS!

"LADOZ," GOLD DRAGON. YOU'RE NOW CLEAR OF INTERLOPERS! YOU CAN GO ON WITH RED LIGHTNING!

THANK YOU, DRAGON! BUT GIVE US COVER UNTIL THE "ORLYONOK" DEPARTS!

NO CAN DO! WE'RE BINGO FUEL! THEY WON'T TRY ANYTHING ELSE TONIGHT, BUT TOMORROW'S LIKELY TO BE A BUSY DAY...

THE "ORLYONOK" IS IN SIGHT!

A FEW MILES AWAY...

NOT A TRACE OF RESCUE 2... THOSE ANIMALS SHOT THEM DOWN!... THIS SO-CALLED MUTINY WAS JUST ANOTHER TRAP! LET'S NOT GET ANY CLOSER. IT'S A GOOD THING THIS HELICOPTER IS VIRTUALLY UNDETECTABLE!

YOU SHOULD HAVE A LOOK IN THE 075... THE DETECTOR SIGNALS A RADAR EMITTING FROM THAT AREA...

075... OK... FOCUSSING... THERE'S SOMETHING, BUT FOR THE MOMENT ALL I CAN SEE IS FOAM...

◎... X 250   B 075 D7.2

IT'S CLEARING UP...? OH?! WHAT IN THE BLAZES IS THIS?!

DESCRIBE IT!

NEVER SEEN ANYTHING LIKE THAT!... IT LOOKS LIKE A JUMBO JET, SEAPLANE VERSION, WITH SHORT WINGS... RING ANY BELLS, IGOR?

B 07   07.0

AN "ORLYONOK"! THEY CALLED IN AN "ORLYONOK"! I WONDER WHAT FOR... IT'S A GROUND EFFECT VEHICLE WITH THE CAPACITY OF A SHIP BUT THE SPEED OF A PLANE...

◎... X 250

IT CAN CARRY UP TO 150 PASSENGERS AT NEARLY 250 MILES PER HOUR, AND HAS A RANGE OF 1000 MILES.

FANCY MACHINE!

A LAUNCH HAS SAILED TO IT... SEVERAL OFFICERS ARE GETTING ABOARD THE GEV... HEY! SOMEONE'S BEING MOVED UNDER THREAT! HE SEEMS TO BE TIED UP... IT'S GOT TO BE BUCK!

ARE YOU SURE?

PRETTY MUCH! THINK... IF WE GO WITH THE THEORY THAT BUCK IS AT THE CENTRE OF THESE RATS' PLANS, AND THEY'RE LEAVING THE SINKING "LADOZ," THEN HE HAS TO BE TAKEN ALONG WITH THEM... THAT MONSTER'S ABOUT TO GET AIRBORNE... FOLLOW IT, TUMB!

SONNY'S RIGHT—DO AS HE SAYS!

I HOPE YOU'RE RIGHT, BECAUSE THE "LADOZ" IS STILL PRETTY USEFUL TO THEM... LOOK AT THE JAMMING WARNING PANEL: LIT UP LIKE A CHRISTMAS TREE... THEY'VE NEVER RADIATED SO MUCH!

50A

IT'S PICKING UP SPEED! WE'RE GOING TO FIND IT DIFFICULT TO KEEP UP... STRANGE, THIS HEADING WILL TAKE US STRAIGHT TO BULGARIA!

LATER, AS THE "ORLYONOK" IS THREATEN-ING TO PUT TOO MUCH DISTANCE BETWEEN IT AND THE "SEAHAWK"...

IT LANDED... LET'S DO THE SAME!

ARE YOU CRAZY, SONNY? WE'RE NOT IN A "SEA KING" (*)!

(*)The SH-3 "Sea King" is an amphibious helicopter.

WHAT ABOUT THE FLOTATION BAGS?

THEY'RE IN CASE OF AN EMERGENCY LANDING AT SEA. I'M NOT SURE WE'D BE ABLE TO TAKE OFF AGAIN AFTERWARDS!

WE DON'T KNOW HOW LONG THEY'RE GOING TO STAY THERE, AND WE HAVE TO CONSERVE FUEL! TRY—OTHERWISE, WE RISK HAVING TO ABANDON BECAUSE OF DRY TANKS!

AND THE NIGHT GOES BY...

GOOD GRIEF! THAT ONE CAME PRETTY CLOSE! PRETTY BUSY AROUND HERE!

WE'RE IN THE MIDDLE OF THE BOSPHORUS-ODESSA ROUTE. THEY CHOSE TO HIDE HERE BECAUSE OF THE AMOUNT OF TRAFFIC!

Francis Bergèse

50B

NEVER-ENDING NIGHT...

... FOR EVERYONE...

ANOTHER ONE!

YOU KNOW FULL WELL THAT TURNING ON THE POSITION LIGHTS COULD GET US SPOTTED!

FINALLY, AT DAWN...

HELL! I THOUGHT I'D NEVER GET OFF THE WATER! JETTISONING THE BAGS... IGOR, LOOK! THE JAMMING HAS STOPPED! TRY CONTACTING THE "KUZNETSOV"!

ABOARD THE "ORLYONOK"...

UNDERWAY AGAIN AT LAST... ABOUT TIME! I WAS RUNNING OUT OF CIGARETTES! YOUR FINAL HOUR DRAWS NEAR, YANKEE!

KNOCK KNOCK KNOCK

...?! WHAT...? IT'S YOU?!

STORNIK IS ASKING FOR YOU ON THE BRIDGE. I'LL GUARD THE PRISONER!

WHAT? HAS HE GONE MAD?! OR YOU'RE LYING!... STORNIK WOULD NEVER LEAVE THE AMERICAN IN THE HANDS...

... OF A STUPID UKRAINIAN LIKE YOU... ARH!

POW POW

POOR TUMBLER... WE'RE ALWAYS SOMEONE ELSE'S STUPID! GREETINGS, COLONEL DANNY. I'M NIKOLAYEV 17!

?!

NIKOLAYEV 17! NOW THE CAST IS COMPLETE! BUT SENATOR SMIGHT...

SMIGHT WOULD STOP AT NOTHING TO COUNTER ADMIRAL FARRELL... BY THE WAY, DIDN'T YOU FIND YOUR ESCAPE YESTERDAY A LITTLE TOO EASY? I HAD TO GIVE YOU A CHANCE TO TURN ON YOUR BEACON...

THANK YOU.

I WAS SURE YOU'D SEIZE THE OPPORTUNITY... BUT WE SHOULD HURRY! WE HAVE TO STOP THIS THING AS QUICKLY AS POSSIBLE!

TAKE THIS AND FOLLOW ME!

YOU SEEM VERY WELL INFORMED, NIKOLAYEV 17. I SUPPOSE THAT COUNTS AS AUTHENTICATION. IN ANY CASE, AT THIS POINT I JUST HAVE TO FOLLOW YOU!

KHARASHO! TWO SUKHOIS WILL JOIN US IN 20 MINUTES. THEY'LL STOP THE "ORLYONOK" BY STRAFING THE MAIN PROPELLER. IT SHOULDN'T ENDANGER OUR FRIEND...

STORNIK AND HIS MEN ARE ON THE UPPER DECK AND HAVE NO REASON TO LEAVE IT FOR NOW. YOUR FRIENDS ARE CHASING US ABOARD THEIR HELICOPTER.

OH?!

WE'LL GO TO THE REAR ELECTRONICS ROOM AND DESTROY THE RELAYS OF THE TURBOPROP'S CONTROL SYSTEM... THERE'S ONE ON EACH SIDE.

IF WE DESTROY BOTH SIMULTANEOUSLY, THE ENGINE WILL SHUT OFF, AND THE TWO TURBOJETS IN THE NOSE WILL BE INSUFFICIENT TO MAINTAIN SUSTENTATION SPEED... HERE WE ARE. YOU TAKE THIS ONE... I'LL GO TO THE OTHER SIDE.

ALL SET...?

READY.

FIRE!

MAYBE THE MOST DECISIVE BULLETS OF MY CAREER! CERTAINLY THE MOST ENJOYABLE! LONG LIFE, COMRADE GORBACHEV!

RESCUE, THIS IS ALBATROSS. WE'RE PASSING YOU NOW... THANKS FOR GUIDING US. WE HAVE THEM NOW!

GO AHEAD, ALBATROSS. BUT DON'T FORGET THAT OUR FRIEND BUCK DANNY IS ABOARD AND THAT WE MUST GET HIM BACK IN ONE PIECE!

HEY! THERE'S SMOKE COMING OUT OF THE AIRCRAFT'S REAR!

IT LOOKS LIKE IT'S LOSING SPEED AND ALTITUDE!

WE'LL LEAVE THROUGH THIS EMERGENCY HATCH... UNHOOK THIS RUBBER RAFT!

IT'LL INFLATE AUTOMATICALLY ON CONTACT WITH THE WATER!

THERE'S ONLY ONE CHANGE TO THE PROGRAM: I MUST STAY AND FIGHT ALONGSIDE MY COMRADES TO TRY AND KEEP THIS TOY FOR UKRAINE! YOU'RE LEAVING ALONE!

!?

ADIEU, COLONEL DANNY! GOD BE WITH YOU!

THIS IS ALBATROSS... THE "ORLYONOK" IS IN THE WATER! I DON'T KNOW WHAT KIND OF MIRACLE THIS IS... IT WASN'T US!

THERE, IN THE RAFT... IT'S BUCK! YIPPEE! I'LL GET ON THE WINCH ASAP! WE'RE GETTING HIM BACK!

THE KAMOVS ARE THERE. THEY'LL TAKE CARE OF THOSE PIRATES!

GOOD LORD, IT'S SONNY! I'VE NEVER BEEN SO HAPPY TO SEE HIM! AND HE'S SO EXCITED HE'S GOING TO END UP IN THE DRINK!

MY FRIENDS! IT'S SO GOOD TO SEE YOU! IGOR, CALL YOUR PEOPLE RIGHT AWAY. STORNIK BRAGGED ABOUT HIS INTENTIONS... HIS ACTIONS ARE PART OF A BIGGER PLAN: A PUTSCH IN MOSCOW!

LATER...

YOU WERE RIGHT: WASHINGTON JUST WARNED US THAT THE RED ARMY HAS BEEN PUT ON ALERT... TANKS ARE HEADING FOR MOSCOW... IT SMELLS LIKE A COUP!

AUGUST 19 MONDAY

I SHARE YOUR OPINION, CAPTAIN. MY COUNTRY IS GOING TO GO THROUGH SOME TROUBLED TIMES. I MUST DO MY DUTY; THEREFORE, I REQUEST TO BE ALLOWED TO GET BACK TO MY SHIP. IF WE WIN, I PROMISE YOU THE COLD WAR WILL BE A THING OF THE PAST!

GOOD LUCK, IGOR! SO LONG, PAL! IS THIS REALLY THE END OF THE ARMS RACE THAT UNDERMINED BOTH OUR NATIONS?!...

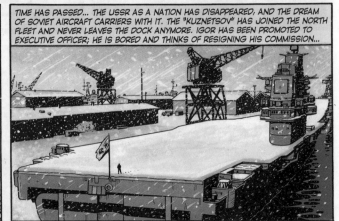

TIME HAS PASSED... THE USSR AS A NATION HAS DISAPPEARED, AND THE DREAM OF SOVIET AIRCRAFT CARRIERS WITH IT. THE "KUZNETSOV" HAS JOINED THE NORTH FLEET AND NEVER LEAVES THE DOCK ANYMORE. IGOR HAS BEEN PROMOTED TO EXECUTIVE OFFICER; HE IS BORED AND THINKS OF RESIGNING HIS COMMISSION...

BUCK AND TUMBLER'S REPORTS HAD CONSEQUENCES: THE US NAVY HAS SHOWN AN INTEREST IN THE "ORLYONOK," AND A RUSSIAN-AMERICAN CONSORTIUM HAS TAKEN OVER ITS DEVELOPMENT. THE US PROTOTYPE IS BEING TESTED AT HAMPTON BASE, VIRGINIA, WHERE ADMIRAL WALKER IS SPENDING HIS HOLIDAYS...

DID YOU SEE, HONEY?... THE POLLS HAD SMIGHT WINNING THE PRESIDENTIAL ELECTION... I'D HAVE HAPPILY VOTED FOR HIM, AND NOW HE'S RETIRING! INCREDIBLE!... QUIET, O'CONNOR!

BOSTON TRIBUNE

SENATOR SMIGHT ABANDONS POLITICS

GRRR... MPFF...

KOHELL (THE END)

SCRIPT: JACQUES DE DOUHET - COLOUR WORK: FRÉDÉRIC BERGÈSE - THANKS TO NIKOLAY TIMOFIEV.